Praise for *Concept Capsules: The Interactive, Research-based Strategies for Teaching Vocabulary*

In the world of teaching, Lisa Van Gemert is not only a pro, but also an expert. Like her other books, *Concept Capsules* reads like a day-long workshop conversation with Lisa right by your side. *Concept Capsules* takes Tier III academic vocabulary and injects the words with strategies for daily practice, daily use, and assessment.

Not only does Lisa share what Concept Capsules are all about, but she shares many of her ready to use Concept Capsules. Furthermore, Lisa offers strategies for assessment of Concept Capsules. Step into the mind of Lisa, as she shares her "secret sauce" for successful delivery of Tier III vocabulary through Concept Capsules.

- Chris Hendricks, Grades 5 – 12 Talented and Gifted Resource Teacher, Foxview Intermediate School, De Pere, Wisconsin

Concept Capsules provides not only the research and pedagogy behind teaching academic language but what Lisa does best in this book is provide context for how to practically use them in the classroom. Beyond that, she provides meaningful explanations for how to create them and explains her "why." Teachers will have no problem implementing this meaningfully into the classroom — especially because she provides examples per content. The practicality is seen again as she discusses how to implement it in ways that won't overwhelm students or the teacher —

this is a key point so many "new ideas" miss! Concept Capsules also meet the need for student driven learning and choice in the classroom. I could see this working out really well in the Blended Learning model I use in my classroom. As an educator, I know that the most important thing for me in any professional learning is the ability to find an immediate takeaway for my classroom and *Concept Capsules* does not disappoint!

- Megan Puckett, M.Ed., Social Studies Department Chair, Bridgeland High School, Cypress, Texas

This book is an essential read for any (and every) teacher, and you cannot say that about most educational books! Another name for it could be *Vocabulary Instruction for Dummies*! Lisa makes the skill of learning Tier III vocabulary easily accessible while generously providing teachers with everything that anyone would need to immediately use this strategy in the classroom including scripts, templates, and researched support. Including all of the research that the methods are based on provides the comfort I need to fully implement this strategy knowing that it is what is best for my students. And it has the added benefit of helping me explain to my students why we are doing things this way, increasing their buy-in.

For as many years as I've known Lisa, I have never seen anything but highly organized, relevant, and poignant lessons coming from her classroom. This strategy is no exception! What I love about the book the most is that she clearly expresses the main goal of the strategy as creating confident students and a positive classroom culture. I'm ecstatic at the thought of providing my students with more equitable footing, more confidence in their knowledge, and even a closer more comfortable bond with me - and with vocabulary of all things! I remain, as ever, in awe of her creativity and ingenuity. Thank you for sharing your gifts with us!

- Rebecca Archer, pre-AP English Teacher & Academic Decathlon Coach, Lamar High School, Arlington, Texas

Lisa Van Gemert's book, *Concept Capsules,* gave me SO much inspiration and a new direction that I *will* use to teach vocabulary this year and beyond! The book does well to explain the "how" and "why" Concept Capsules are an effective tool for students to comprehend and *own* newly presented academic vocabulary. The book also includes tons of examples, ideas, and tips to make Concept Capsules success for every teachers' implementation!

- Dolph Petris, 5th/6th grade, Gifted and Talented Teacher, Rolling Hills Elementary, Fullerton School District, California

Concept Capsules:™

The Interactive, Research-based Strategy for Teaching Academic Vocabulary

Concept Capsules:

The Interactive, Research-based Strategy for Teaching Academic Vocabulary

Lisa Van Gemert, M.Ed.T.

Gifted Guru® Publishing

Gifted Guru® Publishing

Lisa Van Gemert, LLC
P.O. Box 121852
Arlington, TX 76012
permissions@giftedguru.com

Credits:

Artifex https://artifex-graphics.blogspot.com
Deposit Photos: https://depositphotos.com/
Educlips: https://edu-clips.com/
Hidesys Clipart: https://www.teacherspayteachers.com/Store/Hidesys-Clipart
Lovin Lit: https://www.teacherspayteachers.com/Store/Lovin-Lit
Pixabay: https://pixabay.com/
Rebecca B Designs: https://www.teacherspayteachers.com/Store/Rebeccab-Designs
Sarah Pecorino Designs: www.sarahpecorino.com
Teachers Resource Force: https://www.teacherspayteachers.com/Store/Teachers-Resource-Force
The 3am Teacher: http://the3amteacher.blogspot.com/
Unsplash: https://unsplash.com/
Utah Roots: https://www.teacherspayteachers.com/Store/Utahroots
Zip-a-dee-doo-dah Designs: https://www.teacherspayteachers.com/Store/Zip-a-dee-doo-dah-Designs

Cover Design: Okomata

Layout: Rachel Cox

Dedication

To my best friend, Patricia K. Bear:
You have always welcomed all of my words.
Amici Aeternum.

Table of Contents

Section I:
Meet the Method

1

The Concept Capsule Origin Story

You probably picked up this book because you have realized the same thing I have: mastery of academic vocabulary is the secret to success in many domains.

As an elementary teacher, and then a secondary English and Social Studies teacher, I've seen even very strong students felled by their lack of understanding of the language of the discipline they are studying. This was as true of 12th graders as it was for their eight-year-old counterparts in third grade. Not surprisingly, research supports what classroom teachers notice. Studies of elementary students (Baker, S.K., Simmons, D. C., & Kame'enui, 1998) through high schoolers (Cunningham & Stanovich, 1997) consistently show that you can't separate vocabulary from reading comprehension.

I'm a big believer in vocabulary in general, not just in schools, and teachers offer students a tremendous gift when they activate the word curiosity gene in students. A broad vocabulary means you understand wordplay jokes, helps you say what you want to say more precisely (meaning you're more likely to be understood), aids you in learning about your world, engages you more fully in conversations with the best minds in literature, marks you as an educated person, and is a necessary tool for conveying your thoughts in writing. What's not to love?

As a teacher, what's specifically important to me in today's educational environment is that a strong understanding of vocabulary paves the way for serious analysis. As I strive to raise my students' levels of thinking, this has become abundantly clear to me: academic vocabulary is the key building block of critical thinking.

We're not the only ones who've noticed this.

Decades of research demonstrate that vocabulary knowledge is a strong predictor of reading comprehension (Yildirim et al, 2011; Chall & Jacobs, 2003; National Institute of Child Health and Human Development, 2000; RAND Reading Study Group, 2002; Biancarosa & Snow, 2004). You cannot separate the understanding of the words from the understanding of the text as a whole.

We also know that with vocabulary, the rich get richer. What I mean is that the more vocabulary you know, the more you comprehend. The more you comprehend, the more new vocabulary you gain (Stanovich, 1986).

My school's standard vocabulary instruction was based in a mastery of Greek and Latin word pieces, a strategy supported by research (Rasinski, Padak, Newton, Newton, 2011; Pampush & Petto, 2011). I found the knowledge of prefixes, suffixes and roots to be useful personally, as well as professionally. For instance, my orthopedic surgeon was shocked when I understand the structure in my knee he was operating on because I knew that in Latin the root *plico* means "fold."

Even though I was fully committed to this method of instruction for the teaching of vocabulary, I found that it wasn't sufficient for me on a day-to-day basis. It was too slow, and it required an extra step that my students were often unable to take. To be used effectively, it requires students to synthesize the knowledge of different roots, suffixes and prefixes and then apply that synthesis to the word in front of them in real time. Friends, it just didn't always happen.

A staple vocabulary book, *Bringing Words to Life*, persuaded me that I was correct in my intuition about this. The authors agreed, "A robust approach to vocabulary involves directly explaining the meanings of words along with thought-provoking, playful, and interactive follow-up" (3). The authors' own research made sure that students had opportunities to not only use the words, but also to explore different facets of word meanings and apply the words in different ways (84).

I'm also a big believer in the Depth and Complexity framework (so much so that I wrote a book about it with my colleague Ian Byrd), and Language of the Discipline is one of the most commonly used elements in that framework. I needed vocabulary ideas that would fit with pedagogy I wanted (or was required) to use.

As I carefully considered how best to introduce my students to academic vocabulary "robustly," I came to a few conclusions as to best practices. My own classroom experience reinforced what the research I was reading was telling me – academic vocabulary is best explored and mastered when these principles are kept in mind:

- Multiple exposures over time (one-and-done won't work)

- Organic examples that allow for interaction with vocabulary (it can't feel fake)

- Frequent review of all terms (not just the ones you're trying to teach right then)

- Reasonable cadence of exposure to new terms (meaning good pacing)

- Inclusion of invitation to further exploration (luring them into interest in the words outside of how we're using them right now)

- Appropriate use of connection and pattern (the brain loves patterns)

As I came to these conclusions, I knew I needed to change the way I was "doing" vocabulary. I read everything I could find on excellent vocabulary instruction, but there was a problem. Most of it focused on Tier Two vocabulary instruction.

Tier One vocabulary is everyday vocabulary that students will pick up just through living in the world. We don't need to actively teach them what *food* is, for example.

Tier Two vocabulary is the vocabulary we expect educated people to know, but that isn't connected to a particular content area. For example, the word *reflection* is one that we would expect students to know, but not necessarily without instruction. It's not tied to a subject. That's the tier most vocabulary instruction targets. Unfortunately, my students need a lot of Tier Three words – words that are specific to my content area. They needed to know *democracy, allusion, dictatorship, longitude, antebellum,* and others.

I needed something more.

After a few false starts, I came up with the idea of *Concept Capsules.* Concept Capsules are one-page introductions to the academic vocabulary of a discipline, all laid out in the same pattern, shared with students slowly over time and frequently reviewed – what I call in class "playing with." Sound simple? It is!

At first, I called them "Concept Moments," but I changed the name to "Concept Capsules" because I wanted to convey the idea to students that these were small containers with a lot of power behind them, just like space capsules.

As I've facilitated professional development for teachers around the world, I've seen a strong interest in Concept Capsules and how to create and use them. It is clear that many teachers share an understanding of the importance of academic vocabulary and a need for a way to teach it that will capture student interest and result in real understanding.

In this short book I will explain how I choose the words that will become Concept Capsules. I will lay out, word-for-word, the way I introduce the Concept Capsules to my students. I'll show you how to choose which words need Concept Capsules (and which don't). You'll see examples of Concept Capsules and get instructions for how to create your own. You will get 48 Concept Capsules (twelve each from four disciplines). We'll explore how, and more importantly *why*, I frequently quiz my students on Concept Capsules (and why they love it!). We'll end with 25 review activities I use for the Concept Capsules, most of which can be used for other review purposes as well.

In sharing this with you, it is my great hope that you will feel the power of the method and that you will have everything you need to begin implementing it in your classroom right away. I know you'll see great results!

2

How to Use the Concept Capsule Method

Let's talk about how the Concept Capsule strategy works in a classroom. It's so straightforward that it seems impossible that it could be effective (It is, though, I promise!).

In a nutshell, you choose critical vocabulary, explicitly teach it, review it often in ways students enjoy, use it regularly, and quiz it frequently.

I'll share the details of each of those things below, but this is the basic strategy. While there is no one "right" way to do it, here is my general plan:

1. Introduce: Share between three and five new Concept Capsules per week (for a total of about 80 per school year).

2. Review: Play at least one review game or activity per week.

3. Quiz: Give one quiz per week that includes all of the introduced Concept Capsules as possible quiz topics.

4. Include: Include Concept Capsules on every test and quiz, even if it's only one question.

5. Use: Use them in conversation frequently.

6. Test: Give at least one test per semester over all the Concept Capsules.

This constant, integrated approach works with what we know about the neuroscience of learning to increase the chance that the vocabulary is being valued by the students' brains (see Chapter 10 for more about why the quizzes and tests are so important).

Time Commitment

Most educators are concerned about how much time this process takes. It doesn't matter how great something is if you don't have the instructional time to make it happen. Luckily, that's not an issue with Concept Capsules.

The introduction and initial review take about ten minutes per Capsule.

Because you are already giving quizzes and already testing, it does not take extra instructional time to include some Concept Capsule questions. Every test or quiz I give has Concept Capsule questions on it. If the quiz is short, there may be only one.

If I'm assessing student writing, I will integrate a Concept Capsule into the prompt. I could ask them to use a *simile* or *personification* in the response. So, there is not necessarily a question. Rather, there is an application.

Using them in conversation takes no extra instructional time.

The review activities range in time, but they are typically under twenty minutes. The test at the end of the semester is the thing that takes the most time, and it's only twice a year.

So for the things that do take time, where do I find that time?

I use what I call "dead zone" moments to practice Concept Capsules. These are the moments that can be hard to fill with quality instruction. Every classroom is different, but they often arise when you finish an activity and don't have time before the bell to start in on another. They arise when you have a lot of students absent and don't want to move on without them. They can happen when you planned an activity and there's a tech breakdown, making the planned activity impossible. Concept Capsule activities, quizzes, and tests also make excellent emergency sub plans!

Concept Capsules lend themselves beautifully to distance learning. When we are getting students used to online learning and our mannerisms with it, it's helpful to have content that they are familiar with. This ensures that we do not get confused as to what is causing the student difficulty, the tech or the content. Concept Capsule introduction and review are perfect for this. As we get progressively more blended in our classroom instructional modalities, their flexibility will become even more beneficial.

In full honesty, I find that Concept Capsules save me time overall. They increase student achievement, meaning that I have fewer students needing to move to higher levels of RTI. There's a spillover effect here, because the increased self-confidence that comes from success with Concept Capsules often means that students improve in other areas in the class as well. They make acquisition of material much faster.

The real time burden is creating them, and that is done outside of class. (See Chapter 4 for the details on that process.)

Have I persuaded you that you really do have time for them? I hope so!

Step 1: Introduce

The ancient saying, "Well begun is half-done" definitely applies here.

The full explanation of how to introduce Concept Capsules to students is the entirety of Chapter 5 because it's so important.

They must be introduced from a place of encouragement and even excitement. If your attitude is, "Well, here's one more thing they're expecting me to do," your students will feed off that attitude. It's contagious. Consider instead this attitude: "I have found the secret sauce, so get out your little word hamburgers, peeps, because we're gonna douse 'em!" As educators, we often underestimate how much we are the barometer of student attitude. Students read us like they do the weather.

When I explain each Concept Capsule, I make sure to include some anecdote about why I chose it or a cautionary tale about a student who ignored it to his/her peril. I will often create curiosity about the word. Curiosity drives learning, so if I can get them to wonder, I'm half-way there.

I pass out the Capsules, and then we discuss them. I usually take about 5 or 6 minutes to discuss each one. I focus on the definition and sample test question at this time. The extension/interest section below the definition is often explored by the students on their own. Occasionally, depending upon what I included, I will discuss that as well. The section at the bottom is not discussed in class. It is for students to complete on their own. It's where they practice, connect, and explore.

They keep the Concept Capsules in a section of their binders (unless they're digital, of course).

Once they have been introduced to a Concept Capsule, they know it is always fair game. It doesn't matter if they received it in August, we will still be working with it in March.

I do not grade the Concept Capsules. They are for student use. There will be plenty of opportunity for assessment. The Capsules themselves are not a *Gotcha!* If a student wants to check an answer with me from the sample test question or share their extension work with me, I'm happy to do that. I've created keys for the Concept Capsules included in the book that you can view at https://www.giftedguru.com/cckeys.

Step 2: Review

Review games and activities are truly the heart of the Concept Capsule strategy. Chapter 11 goes into 25 of the different games I use and explains the neuroscience of why review is so important. If you are not willing to review, this strategy will not work for you. It is the heart and soul of the method.

After the initial introduction (see Chapter 5 for exactly how to do that), the key idea is that you keep the Capsules in play. Imagine a baseball team warming up, throwing the ball around the bases from player to player, constantly in motion. The ball never really lands anywhere.

That's how Concept Capsules should be: once they're in play, they never get put down. We keep them in motion to keep them front of mind.

For the review to be effective, it cannot be too heavily weighted. It's low-stakes, enjoyable review that is designed to have students feel as successful as possible.

The review activities do not need to be time consuming, but they need to be frequent. It's far better to have frequent, short review experiences than a single, extended experience. In addition to being more effective, it also makes it easier to carve out time for.

The research on this idea has been going on a long time. In the 1880's, Hermann Ebbinghaus conducted a series of experiments (on himself!) to test how quickly people forget learned information. He found that the rate of forgetting was shocking. When plotted on a graph, it looks like this:

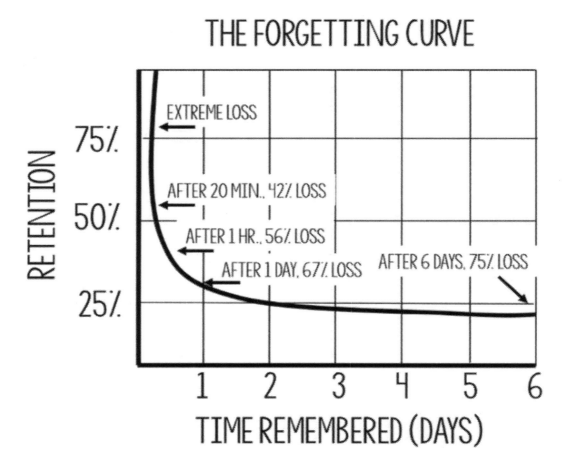

THE FORGETTING CURVE

This type of forgetting is called "transience." Ebbinghaus believed that the key to correcting this curve was repetition. With repeated exposures at optimal times, recall improved dramatically. That curve looks like this:

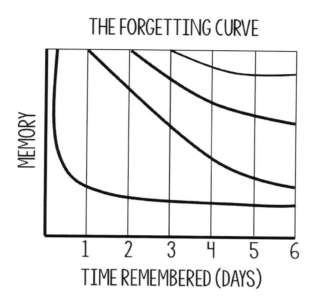

THE FORGETTING CURVE

MEMORY

TIME REMEMBERED (DAYS)

If students have quality review activities that closely follow the initial instruction, the curve is shockingly different. Ebbinghaus believed that every review experience meant you could space further review farther apart (so you need to review less and less frequently as you move on). You do, however, need to review close to initial instruction.

That's the opposite of what most teachers do.

What most teachers do is teach something, assign a practice assignment, perhaps review that assignment, and then move on until there is a test. Then, they give a review of all of that learning.

With Concept Capsules, we review frequently, and we begin the review immediately.

After the introduction of the Concept Capsule, begin reviewing right away. If students have already had a few Concept Capsules introduced to them, I'll take another few minutes and play a review game, including the new Capsule in the game. If this is the first Concept Capsule, practice with just this one by using simple questioning.

For example, if the Concept Capsule is "integer," the teacher would say something like:

- If I say I'm 11 ½ years old, am I using an integer to describe my age?

- If I had $6 and I owe somebody $9, is the amount I need an integer?

- If gas costs $2.39 a gallon, how much more would it have to cost for the price of gas to be an integer?

- I'm a negative whole number. Can I be in the integer club?

- I'm a positive decimal number. Can I be in the integer club?

- Take your age and divide in half. Is that number an integer?

I often ask students to come up with a similar question. I then use those questions to review the next class period (if they're useable). Students love seeing their own questions on the quiz, and not just because they know the answer!

Step 3: Quiz

The quizzes are as important as the review because they are part of the review process. Chapter 10 will dive more deeply into the neuroscience of quizzing and why it's so important. Here, I will discuss what it looks like in class.

Once a week, I will have quick quizzes over the Concept Capsules. These are usually five questions. Sometimes all five questions will be over the same Concept Capsule! The key is that all introduced Concept Capsules can be included on the quiz, not just the ones introduced that week. Once you've learned a new term, that term is fair game for the rest of the year.

These quizzes make excellent sponge activities (bell ringers).

If you prefer, you can tack the questions on to another assessment you're doing, but I have found it's best to have these separate little quizzes as well as including Concept Capsule questions on other assessments.

When I give separate, frequent little Concept Capsule quizzes, I allow students to gain confidence, focus on the vocabulary in isolation for a moment, and build their grades up. Most students do very well on them, so they become a boost in a number of ways.

I do not count the grade for every quiz in isolation. That floods the gradebook and makes the quizzes too high-risk. If there are only five questions, even missing one earns you an 80. Instead, I enter the number correct for each quiz in the gradebook. Once per grading period I will add up all of the questions and give an overall score. If there were 6 quizzes of 5 questions each, I have 30 possible questions. I add up the correct answers and divide by 30 to get a single Concept Capsule Quiz grade that is counted. With digital gradebooks now, it's easy to do that, but before my gradebook could do it, I would use a spreadsheet to calculate that for me.

Occasionally, I will also give a longer Concept Capsule quiz, so that students can practice a lot of Capsules at the same time. (I share an example of one of mine in Chapter 10).

This is not prescriptive. You are free to count the quizzes however you like. I have found that this method works well for my students, but if you're someone who needs to find more things to grade, you could count each one individually.

Step 4: Include

In addition to the dedicated quizzes, consider including one or two Concept Capsule questions on the other quizzes and assessments you give students. Because I want the assessment grade to reflect those objectives, I give these questions as bonus questions. If I forget, my students will ask about them. They look forward to those bonus opportunities!

This accomplishes two things: it keeps the Capsules front of mind, and it keeps students' attitudes about the Capsules positive. They see them as a way to gain extra points.

Another benefit of this is that it provides that frequent review that we learned from Ebbinghaus that we needed.

Feel free to recycle questions. You do not need to come up with 4,000 quiz questions!

Whenever I'm writing a quiz or assessment, I will have at least one or two moments where I need to pause and think of how to write the question. While I'm thinking, I'll just add in a Concept Capsule question. That way, it doesn't feel like an extra piece. It's just part of how I draft the quizzes and assessments.

Students often write great quiz questions, so I always have it as an option on the "What to do if you're done" list for early finishers. If I use their question, I give them a bonus point (in addition to the point they'll get because they know the answer). Once they understand the process, you may never write another question again!

Step 5: Use

When I first became interested in the research behind vocabulary instruction in my pursuit of the vocabulary Fountain of Gold, one of the techniques that came up over and over again seemed too simple to be effective: use the words.

Really? I spent $20 on this book, and all you have to tell me is to use the words? Yes, really.

It turns out that it's pretty common for teachers to give direct instruction about words, but then never use them again except when they test them. They may occasionally say, "Oh, that's one of our vocabulary words!", but it's not a consistent practice.

The research is clear that we need to be immersed in a word ocean, rather than trying to learn by catching a random drip.

How do you do that?

With Tier II words, it's easier to do this than it is with the Tier III words that form our Concept Capsules. It's far easier to find opportunities to use "egregious" in the classroom than "constitutional monarchy." Unless, of course, you're homeschooling in Buckingham Palace.

Some groups of words lend themselves more easily to infusion into regular discussion. If your students are learning weather words or different types of clouds, a simple check in on the day's weather is relatively simple.

When your Concept Capsules are not naturally going to come up in conversation, the techniques that work best for me are analogy and casual reference.

I look for analogies to the Concept Capsules we're using. To stick with the constitutional monarchy example, I look for things we're talking about that could be even the most tangential analogy to the Concept Capsule. I form questions that allow me to discuss the topic at hand, using the analogy of the Concept Capsule I'm targeting. So, I'd say, "How is your textbook like a constitutional monarchy?" or, "Constitutional monarchy is to democracy as pencil is to what?" The crazier, the better. Their responses will shock you with their insight.

I also look for opportunities to throw it out into regular conversation, asking questions such as, "How is our school district like a constitutional monarchy?"

It doesn't take long for this to become second nature. You may even find that your students begin to make suggestions, as well.

Step 6: Test

Once a semester, I give a big Concept Capsule test. As with the quizzes, my students look forward to these as confidence and grade boosters. That always surprises me a little bit because these tests are not easy.

They should resemble as closely as possible the way the students will encounter the term on the most difficult assessment they will see. Try to make these questions more about application and evaluation than knowledge or understanding. The tests are where you pull all the stops. It's where the rubber meets the road. Insert your favorite cliché about really showing what you've got here. That's what these tests should be.

Frequently, students will race to come tell me how "easy" a big test (like an AP® test or our state assessment) felt to them because they had total word confidence. Here's the truth: to the brain, there is no such thing as "easy" or "hard." There is only "familiar" and "unfamiliar." By using the Concept Capsule method, I ensure to the greatest extent possible that my students enjoy a sense of ease so their abilities can shine through.

Wrapping Up

My hope is that by sharing exactly how I implement the Concept Capsule method, you will be able to have a vision for possibilities of how it could work in your class. The method is tried-and-tested, so I would make sure to give it sufficient time to get a feel for it before you start adjusting. Adjust too quickly, and you run the risk of leaving out the step your students need most.

That said, there are no hard-and-fast rules. I created the method, and I'm giving you permission to adjust it any way that works for you.

3

How to Choose Concept Capsules

When I share the Concept Capsule method with teachers, they typically ask three questions:

- How do you choose which words to use?

- How many should you have?

- How long do they take to make?

In this chapter, I'm going to share the answers to the first two questions, and in the next chapter, we'll take a deep dive into making them (and how long it takes).

How Do You Decide Which Words or Terms to Choose?

When I first created the method, I was just choosing words randomly. "Hey, that's a sophisticated word," I'd think. And *boom!* — one Concept Capsule coming up.

Friends, that's not a method.

I needed a reasonable, research-based way to choose. Luckily, it wasn't hard to find one.

A study done in 1987 showed that if you're a mature, literate person, your vocabulary is comprised of three different tiers, or types, of words (Beck, McKeown, & Omanson, 1987). I discussed this in the Origin Story I told in Chapter 1, but I think it's worth revisiting because it applies to all teachers in all disciplines, whether they use this method or not.

According to the study, Tier I words are the words we all use everyday that we don't need to teach students explicitly. They'll just learn them. We don't need to teach the meaning of *fork*, for example. We may have to teach students in early grades how to spell these words, but the meanings are part of their everyday life.

Tier II words are the words that are found in lots of content areas, and without direct instruction, students could easily never know their meaning. These are words like *antidote*, *empathy, gregarious*, or *ubiquitous*. They aren't limited to one content area, but they're unlikely to be understood without their being taught. They are the words educated people know, no matter if that person is a mathematician or a psychologist.

Tier III words are the words that are limited in use or scope. They might be used just in science or just in social studies. Sometimes the frequency of Tier III words is low, but for our purposes, we're going to focus on the idea that these are words that are the academic vocabulary of a discipline.

Key Idea: These are the words the students must understand in order to master the content.

I'm a big believer in the Depth and Complexity framework (as I mentioned, I spent a year of my life writing a book about it). In Depth and Complexity, one of the lenses through which we look at content is called Language of the Discipline. It includes not only the words people use to talk about the domain, but also the tools and people associated with it. For example, *protractor* fits into Language of the Discipline, as does *Euclid*.

Tier III words are the Language of the Discipline. They are words without which students cannot become masters of a discipline.

This fits nicely into the idea of another Depth and Complexity idea: Disciplinarianism. Disciplinarianism is the idea that, to the greatest extent possible, we want our students to approach the content as though they were *disciplinarians*, not just students. We want them to look at math as though they were mathematicians, not just 4th graders. We want them to write essays as if they were authors, not just 9th graders. Tier III words are a large part of what allows that to happen. No one believes someone who says they're a history teacher and doesn't know what the Norman Conquest is. The same is true of many words in many domains.

These are the words that we choose for Concept Capsules. I have an entire website, https://VocabularyLuau.com, that shares resources for teaching Tier II words. Concept Capsules are for Tier III. These aren't spelling words: they're the words students need to master if they are going to move forward as scholars of a subject.

Questions to Ask When Choosing Concept Capsules

There is no specific set of words that are necessary as Concept Capsules because needs change from classroom to classroom. When I am selecting the words and terms to use in Concept Capsules, I ask myself a number of questions:

- **How often will they need to know this word?**

If a word is only in one text we're reading, one lab, one article, or one lesson, it's not a good candidate. If, however, it's a word that we will see and use again and again and again all year, it goes to the top of the list.

- **Is this word likely to show up on a test?**

Even if I'm not teaching the word frequently, sometimes it's a word I know will show up on a standardized test. I have only ever taught tested subjects, and I believe strongly that a student's confidence in approaching and conquering a test is greatly impacted by their mastery of the language they encounter on that test.

- **Will students see this word next year or in subsequent years?**

I may just strike this word a glancing blow, but if I know that next year the students will need to have it mastered, it's a good candidate. This is especially true if I don't have a lot of Concept Capsule words for that content area or course.

- **Is it necessary to understand this word in order to understand other important words?**

I call these *gateway words*. These are the words that you need to know to understand other words. For instance, you can't really understand *isosceles* if you don't understand *triangle*. You can't understand *heavy metal* or *noble gas* if you don't understand *Periodic Table of the Elements*.

- **Do students frequently misuse or misunderstand this word?**

Some words cause confusion. They may be used one way in one content area and a completely different way in another. They may have etymology that makes them confusing. Consider, what really is the connection between *pedestrian* and *pediatrician*? (There is one, actually, but it's odd, is it not?)

One example that comes to mind is *proscribed*. I use this word in social studies frequently. It means forbidden, especially by law. However, it looks and sounds a lot like *prescribed*, which is very nearly the opposite. Confusing word? You're going to the front of the line.

- **Will they learn it without explicit instruction?**

If the word is crucial to know, but you know that you will teach it fully without making it a focus, don't make a Concept Capsule for it. For instance, in my geography class, *map* is an essential word. However, I don't create a Concept Capsule for it because we're going to be using that word almost every day in so many ways that you'd have to work hard to miss it.

Where Do You Find the Words?

I usually start by looking through my textbook's glossary, scanning released versions of the test(s) my students are taking, and reviewing final exams and essays. I search "6th grade math vocabulary" (or whatever it is I'm looking for ideas for) and glance over the lists. I carefully look at the standards for my content. That's a great place to find dates and people, as well as standard vocabulary.

I begin making a list of possible Concept Capsules, and I let my mind stew about it for a while. I find that as I do so, ideas come to me.

While it's important to choose solid Concept Capsules, it's not the end of the world if you realize later that you chose the wrong ones. A little vocabulary never hurt anyone, and you can always make adjustments next year. In fact, my mantra as a teacher has long been, "There's always next year!" If you really feel like you've made a super poor choice, you can pull a Capsule and replace it. You're the teacher, so you can change the rules.

How Many Concept Capsules Should You Have?

The short answer is that I typically use about 80 Concept Capsules through an entire year.

I've tried creating more than that, and it didn't work. They become unwieldly. They make binders too thick. They lose their "specialness" as important words. I have to introduce them to students too quickly. So, 80 has become my personal limit.

When you think about it, 80 is not that many. If you're an elementary teacher with all four main content areas, that's only 20-ish Concept Capsules per content area. If you're a secondary teacher teaching a one-semester class, that's only 40 or so.

If you do not have 80, it's fine to do fewer. Even if you only have ten, that's fine. It's also fine to be very uneven in their distribution. If you're teaching all content areas, it's fine to have 30 math Concept Capsules, 10 language arts, 35 science and 5 social studies, if that's what fits your grade level and students.

Wrapping Up

While choosing which Concept Capsules to create is important, don't get hung up on choosing the exact words you need. You will change them over time, adding in some and removing others. This is normal. Needs change as standards, testing, and methods do. The most important thing is to begin!

4

How to Create a Concept Capsule

Since I made up the strategy, I'll start with giving you permission to make them any way you like. I'll share my method with you in detail, and you are free to use any or all of the method. You're also welcome to completely change it.

My own method has changed over time. When I knew I was going to write this book, I hunted around to see if I could find one of my old Concept Capsules I created when I first started using them. Friends, it wasn't pretty.

You can see in this example of my first one that I started out calling them a "Concept Moment." I think I switched to Concept Capsule in 2009. I've got a definition and how it looked on a test, but that's it.

Here's what's amazing: as bad as they were, they *still* made a huge difference!

Now, I follow the same layout with every Concept Capsule, no matter what the content area or grade level is.

I create them on letter-sized paper (I'll discuss doing them digitally at the end of this chapter). I print them in black and white because I print them on super bright paper. My students know that they need to keep track of them because that paper is expensive, and I do not give extra copies away if they lose theirs. I do make them available for them to print their own, but when Mrs. Van uses her allowance to buy Astrobright® paper, only the bravest would ask for another copy on her paper!

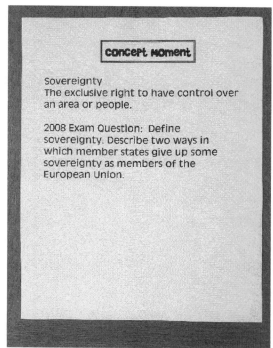

concept moment

Sovereignty
The exclusive right to have control over an area or people.

2008 Exam Question: Define sovereignty. Describe two ways in which member states give up some sovereignty as members of the European Union.

I started using the bright paper because using a color printer was so expensive, but I wanted color. You can group them by color when you do that (all the landforms on yellow, all the formuI

If you use a digital format (again, I'll address that at the end of the chapter), you can have color in the Concept Capsule because it's not being printed.

There are four sections to each Capsule, and I'm consistent in the layout because it makes it so much faster to create them. As I'm thinking about what to put in, or searching the internet or texts for ideas, I keep in mind what those sections are, so I know if I need or can use the information I find.

Of course, you are free to adjust or even completely change the layout, but it will likely help you to see it laid out the way that I do it. You can then adjust the plan to meet your needs. Remember: you are free to adapt and riff off the idea.

In this book, I've included 12 Concept Capsules for each of the four core content areas, but they are not prescriptive. They're just options and examples for you.

Let's look at an example, and then let's take it apart, one section at a time. Because I used the four core content areas for the examples in the book, I'll choose another content area – computer science – for this example.

DEFINE: SERVER

- a computer that is specially equipped with hardware and/or programs that make it possible to serve other computers (called "clients") on its network
- a computer that supplies client stations (other computers) with access to resources (like files or the web) on a computer network
- multiple kinds (e.g., file server, print server, web server, application server)
- Think of it like a waiter. A waiter is also called a server, and waiters bring you things. They connect you to your food & beverages. They help you pay for your meal. Computer servers are kind of like that. They serve other computers.

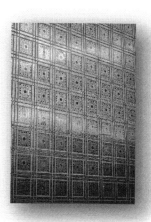

Servers can be clustered, meaning that lots of servers work together to do one service. Here, these servers are all stacked up. Looks like a lot of servers, doesn't it? Some companies have amazing numbers of servers. For example, Microsoft® has over one million servers.

Try this at home, kids! You can build your own server if you've been saving your allowance. This YouTuber will show you how: https://bit.ly/build-a-server.

What It Looks Like on A Test:

Which of the following statements are true of servers? Circle the number of all that apply.

1. It is a satellite of a computer network that feeds off the network.
2. It is a computer that does all the work for another computer (as its servant).
3. It is a computer that hosts data for other computers.
4. It can connect other computers to the internet or to printers.

You're the salesman! Imagine that you have created a company that designs and builds servers. You're going to be competing with big companies like Dell® and IBM®, so you need to offer something special. Write three lines of ad copy to run in a magazine for computer geeks (like you) that share the features you offer.

_____

_____

_____

Concept Capsule Section 1: The Definition

The first section of the Concept Capsule is the definition. In all caps, I type "DEFINE: TERM." Below that, I share the definition using bullet points to make even long definitions easily digestible.

In this case, there are four bullet points. If the point is a full sentence, I start with a capital letter. If not, I don't. I don't worry about mixing them.

DEFINE: SERVER

- a computer that is specially equipped with hardware and/or programs that make it possible to serve other computers (called "clients") on its network
- a computer that supplies client stations (other computers) with access to resources (like files or the web) on a computer network
- multiple kinds (e.g., file server, print server, web server, application server)
- Often, servers are designed to more powerful and reliable than a typical computer, so they are more expensive than a regular computer.

The reason I format it with "define" and then the colon is that if they search it that way on Google, the definition is what they'll find. If you just search "delta" on Google, you get the airline, not the landform. To guarantee they'll find the definition, using this search phrase works. I lay out the Concept Capsule this way to help them learn how to find definitions on their own.

When I'm constructing a definition, I consider a number of variables, including:

- the sophistication of the students (influences word choice and definition length)
- how deeply they need to understand the term
- important examples
- if there are similar terms that might be confused
- if there are related terms (e.g., "It is the opposite of _____.")
- interesting trivia connected to it (often ends up in Section 2)
- etymology

I begin with the basic definition the level I find necessary. You can see in this example that I felt the need to give two definitions to start. That happens when something may have multiple, accurate ways to describe it that are both important to understand. You'll see it in some of the other examples in the book as well.

In the example here, we see that I needed to embed another term, *client*, in the definition.

If the etymology helps clarify or might make it easier to remember, I'll add that in. Here, I debated making the connection between servers and waiters. At first, I didn't, and I had something else (shown in this snippet). I decided that the visual image of a waiter bringing a computer something was powerful, so I changed it.

I will read dozens of definitions as I construct the way I'm going to define it. Remember that dictionaries are copyrighted, so I do not ever take a phrase or definition from somewhere else. Sometimes, it's unavoidable because the definition is so narrow that it's just a fact in the common hive mind. For example, "whole numbers" or "simile" have limited different ways to describe them, so there's bound to be overlap. The main point is, I don't plagiarize the definitions, even for use in my own class. I find that I understand the term (even familiar terms) better if I have reworded the definition and really considered it.

Concept Capsule Section 2: Extension

I put a line below the definition. I usually use dashes, but you can have a solid line. It's up to you. The next section is where I extend learning. The research is clear about how important it is to integrate newly acquired vocabulary into a broader schema and to make connections to known and/or interesting information. That's what this section is all about.

I will almost always have an image on the left, along with an explanation of what the image represents or why it's important. Here, you can see that I found an image of a server cluster, and I'm explaining what it is. I also added in some trivia (Microsoft has over a million servers).

Servers can be clustered, meaning that lots of servers work together to do one service. Here, these servers are all stacked up. Looks like a lot of servers, doesn't it? Some companies have amazing numbers of servers. For example, Microsoft® has over one million servers.

Try this at home, kids! You can build your own server if you've been saving your allowance. This YouTuber will show you: https://bit.ly/build-a-server.

Trivia is key. Most of your students will notice it. I didn't realize when I first started that this would be a thing, but as Concept Capsules became my vocabulary method, it came up again and again. I would overhear students remarking about it to other students. I would hear them telling other teachers. I saw it pop up in their answers on tests and quizzes. They like trivia.

On the right side, I try to find some point of extension. This may be a video to watch, an interesting example, a place to learn more, or any other way I can find to get kids caring about or interested in this concept.

I have a few resources that are important in this process. I use https://bit.ly to shorten the links. I like this site because it free, it lets me customize the link, it lets me tag the links, and it lets me track them. The analytics are amazing. I can tell how many students went to that link and when. It's a beautiful thing.

Images are key in this section, and I use these sites most of all:

- Pixabay (https://pixabay.com)

- Unsplash (https://unsplash.com)

- Rawpixel (https://rawpixel.com)

- Morguefile (https://morguefile.com)

- For math and science terms, I often purchase clipart on TeachersPayTeachers (https://www.teacherspayteachers.com)

Even if I'm using just the Capsule in my class, I make sure to get copyright-free, royalty-free images. If I can't find what I need on these sites, I will use Google® to search for an image, employing the tool to search by usage license.

Here, I was searching for an image of the Sagrada Familia cathedral in Barcelona. I searched it on Google, chose "Images," clicked on Tools (see it there on the right just under the search bar?), chose "Usage Rights," and then checked "Labeled for Reuse."

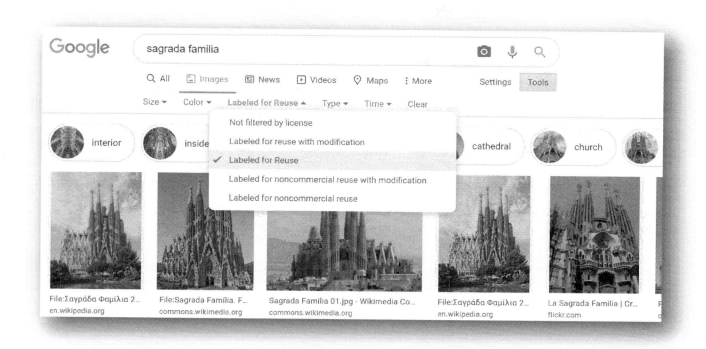

The point is that we as educators should lead by example in respecting copyright. "Fair Use" is not nearly as broad as we like to think!

Thinking of what to put in Section 2 can be tricky, but often, as I mentioned above, this is where the trivia ends up. I usually find this as I'm hunting down definition ideas, but if not, I just search for "trivia about integers" or "examples of obtuse angles in real life." I've been known to tear pages out of magazines in doctors' offices if I see something I think I can use. Please don't tell!

Section 2 is my favorite part to create. It's where I have a lot of fun. It's the part that I think starts to separate this method from any other. Have a good time with it! Don't hesitate to make it weird or wacky or off-the-wall. The crazier, the better, actually. The more odd or interesting it is, the more likely it will be to engage your students.

Concept Capsule Section 3: How It Looks on a Test

Even in my original (humble) example I showed you, I had an example of the term used on a test. Early on I realized that students absolutely had to know what the term might look like when they were tested on it. This has proven to be equally true of my youngest students as it is of my AP® students.

The crucial part of this section is to give an example of the type of question they'll see. It's not just the content itself that's important: it's also the *manner* in which the question will be asked. Sometimes, I even give two examples of this.

What It Looks Like on A Test:

Which of the following statements are true of servers? Circle the number of all that apply.

1. It is a satellite of a computer network that feeds off the network.
2. It is a computer that does all the work for another computer (as its servant).
3. It is a computer that hosts data for other computers.
4. It can connect other computers to the internet or to printers.

At higher levels of student sophistication, I give trickier questions. You can see here that answer choice 2 is a distractor. I use the idea of "servant," which they have associated with server, but the answer itself is incorrect.

To find the sample test questions, the first place I go is to the highest stakes test they will find for this content. If they're an AP student, I look at released tests or sample questions from test prep books. If there's a state assessment, I'll look there. If they'll see it on the SAT® or ACT®, I'll pull a question from there. If it's my own assessment, I'll use a question from there.

Obviously, if I use my own question, I will change it up a bit so that when they encounter that test, they don't have it memorized.

Here's the main idea: *match the thinking level of the question you share to the thinking level of the questions they will encounter*.

If they're going to see a bunch of application opportunities, but you've only shared knowing and understanding level questions, you've got a big disconnect.

This is a key section, so please don't skip it. When students have a strong awareness of the level to which they need to understand and be able to apply a concept, the more able they are to make the decision to devote sufficient time to acquiring that needed knowledge. If they only see simple samples, they won't work hard enough.

Concept Capsule Section 4: Work with the Concept

The fourth and last section is where I have students work with the concept. I put in an engaging activity that they can interact with. This is the part I think about longest. I really have to consider what I think they can do that will get this word past the gatekeeper of their memories.

I keep a larger-size sticky note at my desk with the list of the most common ideas I use to help me remember my go-to options.

I try not to be too same-y with them because variety is important, but when you're just getting started, do whatever you can think of! Don't put too much pressure on yourself to come up with the most amazing idea ever.

> You're the salesman! Imagine that you have created a company that designs and builds servers. You're going to be competing with big companies like Dell® and IBM®, so you need to offer something special. Write three lines of ad copy to run in a magazine for computer geeks (like you) that shares the features you offer.
>
> _____
>
> _____
>
> _____

In this example, you can see that I gave them a scenario. That's one of the options I use. Here are some of the others:

- Wordsearches (I create them at https://wordsearchlabs.com.)

- Crosswords (I create them at https://crosswordlabs.com.)

- Circle the Words – I put in a list of words, and they circle the ones that go with the target word

- Fill-in-the-Blank

- Fallen Phrases (Use: http://puzzlemaker.discoveryeducation.com.)

- Real-life Application (including scenarios, like the one above)

- Hidden Message (Use http://puzzlemaker.discoveryeducation.com.)

- Analogies

- Synonym/Antonym

- Sketching

- Letter Tiles (Create at: http://puzzlemaker.discoveryeducation.com.)

- Matching

You'll see dozens of examples in the sample Concept Capsules included in the book, and you'll quickly get a feel for them. Section 4 is the last section, so now your Concept Capsule is complete!

Creating Concept Capsules Digitally

Can you create these digitally and save all that glorious Astrobright paper? Absolutely. To do so, simply use whatever tool you want (probably Google Docs or Slides would be easiest) to replicate the layout. The beauty of that method is that you can use all the color you want. Ah, color. It makes me happy just thinking about it.

One of the key ingredients is that interactive piece in section 4, so make sure that you have a way for students to actually engage and interact with the Capsule. Switching it to a digital format should not mean that it just becomes something to read. They must be able to engage with them.

If you're going to use Google Slides, my suggestion would be to resize the slide to the size of a piece of paper so that they can be printed, should you or a student so desire.

Another possibility is to make them available to students both digitally and in print. We know that comprehension is (much, much) better in print than on devices, so it's possible you will find that some students greatly benefit from the printed version to truly understand the term.

If you'd like a template for a digital version, I created one in Google Slides. It's available to you when you join in the Concept Capsule Insiders, the free email source of Concept Capsule Goodness.

It's available at https://vocabularyluau.com/template.

How Long Does It Take to Create a Concept Capsule?

So, how long *does* it take to complete this process? I feel guilty even writing this, but it really does depend. If you're very, very familiar with the word and the ideas flow, it can be shockingly quick to produce one (maybe 15 – 20 minutes). If you have to look around and consider and massage and think…well, let's just say I've had them take a couple of hours. I hate typing that, but I need to be honest with you.

Here are some ideas to make that process manageable:

- Divide and conquer. Find some friends who teach what you teach and share the wealth! Come up with terms you're going to use (Chapter 3), and then divide up the Capsules. Share them amongst yourselves when you're done.

- Spread it out! Create ten or so over the course of a summer. Use those for a year, then add ten more the next summer.

- Justify your Netflix® addiction and create them while your binge-watching you fave show. Warning: It takes longer if you do it while watching something, but sometimes it makes it feel less like work.

- Create them by section, working on them in small moments of opportunity (waiting at a soccer practice, waiting for a faculty meeting to start [!], when you have a spare five minutes and don't feel like dragging out a lot of stuff).

- Divide and conquer. Avoid thinking that you need to create the entire Capsule. Just think of them in terms of a single section. You don't need to find time to make a whole one. You only need time to make a section or at least work on a section.

- Batch process them. Consider doing several wordsearches or crosswords or fallen phrases while you're on a particular website.

- Chapters 6 – 9 of this book share a dozen examples from each of the four core content areas. You can use those, of course!

You may find that you love the strategy, but the time to create the Capsules is burdensome. That's okay! You can purchase other ready-made Concept Capsules at my Teachers Pay Teachers store for a very, very reasonable price, and I'll be adding more, so feel free to follow along! (https://www.teacherspayteachers.com/Store/Giftedguru). I'm always trying to think of terms that would help teachers, so feel free to email suggestions to lisa@giftedguru.com.

You are welcome to share ones you create with other teachers, but you may not sell those, as "Concept Capsule" is a trademarked term.

Wrapping Up

Creating the Concept Capsules is the most time consuming part of the entire method. Once created, you can use the same ones year after year, so it's an investment. You will find a groove, and I think you will find the process becomes enjoyable over time. You will find the method that works best for you, and when you see the benefits your students enjoy, you will think that time was time very well spent.

5

Introducing Concept Capsules to Students

I'm a big believer in the power of a good introduction. If you've ever felt out of place at a party because you didn't know anyone, you know what I mean. All it takes is for someone to introduce themselves to make you feel more at home and comfortable. It can change your entire opinion about the party.

The same dynamic exists with students and classroom strategies at an even deeper level. We need to get kids to buy in to the power in the strategy in order for it to be effective. They have to believe in its ability to help them.

This isn't just a good idea. The science backs it up. In his book *Maximum Brainpower: Challenging the Brain for Health and Wisdom*, neuroscientist Shlomo Breznitz explains how hope and despair are powerful and can be manipulated (shockingly easily). He tested his theory on optimism/pessimism on a large group of soldiers. It's super interesting, so I'm going to share what he did. As you read about it, consider what it tells us about classrooms.

After a full year of soldier-y training, the soldiers marched across the desert with full packs and gear. In the Army, we call this "rucking" (Yes, I was in the Army). The study wanted to see what (if any) impact the soldiers' psychological state had on the soldiers' physical performance. The soldiers were all going to be marching 40 kilometers (25 miles). The difference was in *what they were told they would be doing.* They were told either that they would be a) marching 40 kilometers (the accurate amount), or b) marching 30 kilometers, c) marching 60 kilometers, or d) not told anything.

The soldiers' performance varied widely based on what they were told. It was shocking, really. The group that did best? The group that was told the accurate distance (40km). Next came the optimistic group who thought they were only going 30km. The soldiers who weren't told how far they were going came in third, and the last place group were the soldiers who were told they'd be marching 60km. One third of them dropped out after only 10km! That's crazy because those soldiers could do 10km easily. The study's designers had planned to tell them the correct distance at 29km, but it didn't do much good because so many had already quit.

As teachers, I think we need to consider the implications of this study for our classrooms. We sometimes think that the more information the better. We have a big, high-stakes test at the end of the year, so we'd better warn kids about it all year. After all, if they don't pass, there are serious consequences. But this study turns that idea on its head. What made you most likely to succeed was when what you thought you would face bore a strong resemblance to what you *did* face.

The soldiers who weren't told how far they were going or who were told an inflated number let their minds trump their physical ability. In the study, they took blood samples and found that it affected the levels of stress hormones in their bodies. Their belief in themselves manifested itself on a cellular level. In his book, Breznitz writes, "[T]he brain does not want the body to expend its resources unless we have a reasonable chance of success…If we do not believe we can make it, we will not get the resources we need to make it…Both hope and despair are self-fulfilling prophecies" (157).

The study was so fascinating that when I first read about it, I couldn't stop thinking about it (I strongly recommend reading the book). I was thinking about students who didn't think they could do the work or who didn't know exactly what the work (or test) would entail. I wondered how often the dynamic described in the study affected my kids.

I wondered how often students who thought the challenge would be more difficult than it actually was gave up months before the actual test. I wondered how many had no clue what was really going to be expected of them. I knew that Concept Capsules could move my students in the same way knowledge had moved the soldiers. The research is clear that vocabulary helps comprehension (as discussed in the Introduction). If I tell you that I have a technique that's been shown to help you master vocabulary so that you'll be able to know what you need to in order to do well on the test, Breznitz's study seems to argue that you'll do better.

I try to give my students an accurate assessment of whatever they are facing. I don't sugar coat it, but I also don't build it up so much that I undermine them. Part of this means that I take time to onboard students to the idea of Concept Capsules, why I'm using them, and what they can do for the students. I take a little time to get them to buy in to the idea that they will face a challenge and there is a strategy that will help them meet that challenge.

Introducing the Concept Capsule Method

I'm sharing with you (word-for-word) how I introduce the method to my students. I introduce them to the idea of academic vocabulary and its importance. I introduce the

Concept Capsule method, and I share the first two Concept Capsules. I use this exact same method no matter what grade level the students are, but of course, you are free to adjust this in any way you like. Ready? Let's go!

Say: *Just think the answer to this in your mind: Which of these words would you expect to hear from a doctor, "prescription" or "swimming pool?"*

Which of these words would you expect to hear at the grocery store, "milk" or "car"?

These were simple questions, weren't they? They were simple because we are familiar with what words go with what places and people and professions.

If you went to a doctor for a broken arm, and she said, "Oh, that bone in your arm is broken. I don't remember what that bone is called, but I know exactly how to fix it," would you believe her?

If you meet a new friend who says he plays soccer but can't name the position he plays, would you think he played very much?

Think for ten seconds about why it is important to know the words for things if you want to be taken seriously.

[After ten seconds, call on students for responses.]

Words that are specific to a job or a sport or a class in school are called "academic vocabulary" or the "language of the discipline." Sometimes in textbooks, these words will be in bold type. Sometimes, you'll find these words and their definitions in the back in what is called the "glossary."

[If your textbook has bolded words and/or a glossary, pull it out and explore a few of the words you find there. If not, move forward.]

Some words are the same, no matter what you're talking about. There are lots of everyday words that we use at doctor's offices and grocery stores and on vacation and in math class.

[Do a rapid-fire brainstorm of "Everyday Words" students know. These will vary, so just accept anything reasonable. Divide students into groups of three or five. Give each group a copy of the Venn Diagram below.]

Each of your groups has a Venn Diagram with two circles, one labeled "Everyday Words" and one labeled "Academic Vocabulary." Think about how these words are the same and how they're different. As a group, complete the diagram with characteristics of the two types of words, and where the circles overlap, share characteristics of both types of words. You have five minutes to come up with as many ideas as possible.

[After five minutes, bring the class back together. Display the Venn Diagram to the class using a document camera or Smart Board. Ask each group for one idea from each of the three spaces, filling out the diagram as you go. It's best to ask this in a random pattern, one circle at a time, rather than having one group list their three words in a row. Discuss where the responses are similar and where they are different. If your students are very young, you can do this orally.]

One of the reasons academic vocabulary is important is to save time. If a doctor had to say, "I'm going to give you a piece of paper for you to take the pharmacy so they know what medicine to give you and how much of that medicine you need and how often you should take it," it would take a lot more time than saying, "I'm going to give you a prescription."

In order to talk about what we're learning, we need to agree on what words we'll use and what those words mean.

This isn't just for this class. All scholars must know the vocabulary of their discipline. A "discipline" is an area of study, and people who study that area seriously are called "disciplinarians." We are disciplinarians, too, so we use the words of our discipline.

On a scale of one to five, five being most important and one being not at all important, how important do you think academic vocabulary is to being successful in what you are studying?

[Either discuss or (preferred) have students line up in the order of importance they choose, with one side of the classroom being a one and the other side being a five.]

A famous American author named James Michener wrote novels about places and their history. One of the places he wrote about was the Chesapeake Bay near Washington, D.C. [If you have a map, show where Chesapeake Bay is.]

In the novel, Michener described how a man who wanted desperately to be a boat builder, but was held back because he didn't know the vocabulary of the discipline.

[Using a document camera or a Smart Board, display the quote below. Two versions of the quote are provided, one with unfamiliar words defined and one without. Use whichever you prefer or show the one with definitions first, and then re-read without definitions.]

Thinking back to our scale of one to five about the importance of academic vocabulary, how important do you think this carpenter thinks the language of the discipline is.

[Either discuss or (preferred) have students line up in the order of importance they choose, with one side of the classroom being a one and the other side being a five.]

To help us share our ideas in this class, we'll use academic vocabulary, and we're going to learn much of it using something called Concept Capsules. Concept Capsules are one-page sheets that have the definition of the word and more. We'll be getting new Concept Capsules throughout the year, and you get your first two today.

[Distribute the first Concept Capsule.]

We're going to look at this one first for its format as well as its meaning because all of the Concept Capsules will be laid out in the same way.

First, at the top you'll see the word "define" followed by a colon and the word. It's that way because when you are using a search engine to find the definition of a word, you will get that definition if you search using that format, "define, colon, word." If you just search the word "delta," for example, you would get the airline. If you want to know what a delta is, meaning the landform, you need to use define, colon, delta.

Next, you'll see the bullet points below. Those are where you'll always find the definition of the word.

Below that, look to the left side of the paper. Here you will always see a picture of some kind. It may be a diagram, or it may be an image.

Opposite that, you will see an extra something. It's an extension invitation to learn more about the word. In this class, we learn for more reasons than just a grade. We learn because it's fun. We learn to have a richer life. So, if you would like to learn more, this is where you'll find that.

Below that, notice the box. This box contains a question representing how the word could appear on a test. This isn't the actual test question, but it is an example of how one could look.

Lastly, you will see some kind of activity. It may be a puzzle. It may be a word scramble. It may be an opportunity to connect the word to our lives. Sometimes you'll do that on your own, and sometimes we'll discuss it together.

[Go over this Concept Capsule now specifically, discussing its definition, the connected image, the extension invitation, the test question, and the activity. Distribute and discuss the second Concept Capsule in the same way.]

Now we're going to play a little game with the two Concept Capsules we've got. [Choose any of the Review Games marked with an asterisk in the Review Games.]

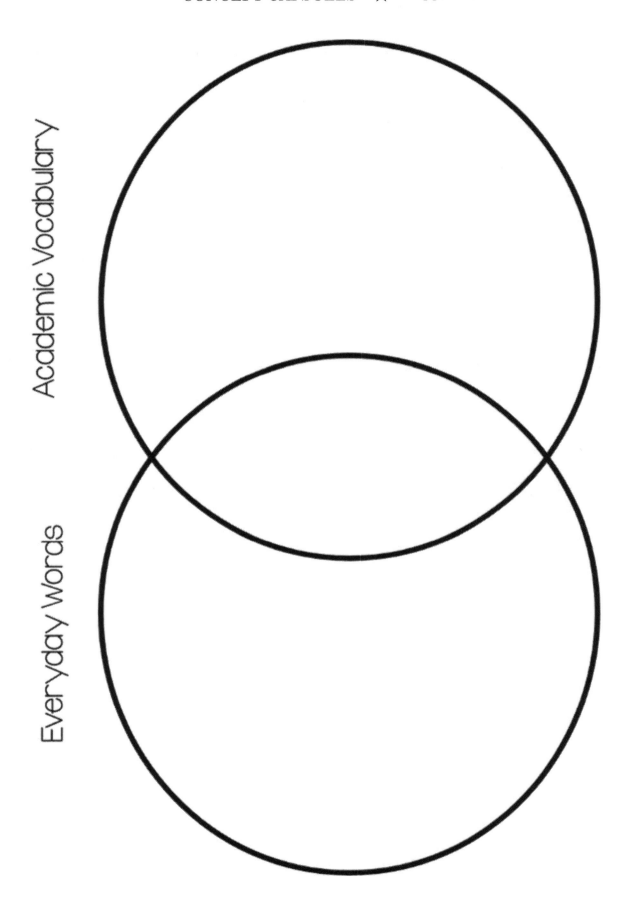

Academic Vocabulary

Everyday Words

"But always he lacked the essential tool without which the workman can never attain (reach) true mastery: he did not know the names of any of the parts he was building, and without the name he was artistically incomplete. It was not by accident that doctors and lawyers and butchers invented specific but secret names for the things they did; to possess the name was to know the secret. With correct names one entered into a new world of proficiency (expertise, to be accomplished at something), became the member of an arcane (mysterious or secret) brotherhood, a sharer of mysteries, and in the end a performer of merit. Without the names on remained a bumbler (someone who makes mistakes because they don't know) or, in the case of boatbuilding, a mere carpenter."

James Michener, *Chesapeake*

"But always he lacked the essential tool without which the workman can never attain true mastery: he did not know the names of any of the parts he was building, and without the name he was artistically incomplete. It was not by accident that doctors and lawyers and butchers invented specific but secret names for the things they did; to possess the name was to know the secret. With correct names one entered into a new world of proficiency, became the member of an arcane brotherhood, a sharer of mysteries, and in the end a performer of merit. Without the names on remained a bumbler or, in the case of boatbuilding, a mere carpenter."

James Michener, *Chesapeake*

Introducing Individual Concept Capsules

To some extent, introducing the Concept Capsules was discussed in Chapter 2. Here, I'd like to dive a little more deeply into it because it's just that important. If you have 80 or so capsules for a year, you will repeat this process 80 times, so it's important to have a handle on how to do it.

I print mine on colored paper to signal how important they are. You can use other techniques to signal how special they are. Here are a few suggestions:

- Have a Concept Capsule song you play whenever you're going to reveal a new one.

- Ring a bell or play a drumroll (you can find these sounds on your phone) when it's time.

- Wear a special piece of headgear, like a hat or crazy headband.

- Use special lighting.

- Give out a chart that they add a sticker to every time they get a new Capsule.

- Share a small food item (if allowed). I've used a single round oat piece of cereal! (Isn't it crazy what students think is cool?)

Whatever you choose, find a way to make it special. In addition to giving students a shot of dopamine, it helps to build a class culture. When I ask former students what they remember most about the class, inevitably they will mention Concept Capsules. They become a part of who we are as a class. This is largely true because of making their introduction a special moment.

As you go through the Concept Capsule, touch on each section individually, rather than just passing it out and saying, "Here you go! You're responsible for it now!"

A friend of mine (who is an excellent teacher) told me that she tells students that they are responsible for all of the vocabulary they encounter in the books they read, but she provides no direct instruction for it. That is an unacceptable and ineffective practice.

We're being deliberate and very, very intentional about these terms. After all, we picked them because we know they are necessary for student achievement. We are going to take the time it deserves (and it's really only about five or six minutes), to go over the definition, explain anything from the second section that they need to know, explain how to answer the sample test question, and give any extra instructions for the interactive section at the bottom of the sheet.

This process will be the same if the format of the Capsule is digital.

Once it's introduced, begin review right away, as I described in Chapter 2. Now, that Capsule goes into the rotation and becomes the subject of quizzes, review activities, and gets mentioned in class.

One important note: I do not try to tie the introduction of the Concept Capsule to when it will be needed in a lesson. I've tried this, but it didn't work. What happened was that some units had loads of Capsules, while others had none. I needed to space them out steadily, not flood students with a dozen at a time. I do try to make sure I introduce the term before it's needed. So, students may be introduced to a term months before they see it in a lesson.

Wrapping Up

The introduction of the method and the individual capsules is essential. When done well, students will clearly understand the importance of the terms, as well as what they mean. Done poorly, you will face opposition and resentment. They will become a chore instead of a source of energy and even excitement. Take the time to introduce them, and that investment will pay off tenfold.

Section II:
Concept Capsule Samples

You've already seen a full example in Chapter 4 where I described how to create Concept Capsules. Now, you will see 48 more examples from the four core content areas: ELA, Math, Science, and Social Studies.

I selected them from a range of grade levels and topics, hoping to share examples that would give teachers a feel for what they might look like in your specific classroom.

Interestingly, they work across a wide range of grade levels, meaning that I could use the same Concept Capsule with a fourth grade student as I would with a ninth grade student.

My suggestion would be to look through all 48, even the ones you know you would never use. You will get ideas for creating your own as you see example after example of what they can look like. Pay attention to what you like and dislike about the different Capsules, so that you create your own list of possible layouts, sections ideas, and style choices.

While these examples are for the core content areas, hopefully you saw from the computer science example in Chapter 4 that they work equally well in other domains.

You are free to use these examples in your classrooms. You are also free to ignore them and create your own style. One reminder: these cannot be shared on any information storage and/or retrieval system (including Google Classroom®, Blackboard®, Moodle®, or similar platforms). Unfortunately the security of documents has not kept pace with the ability to share them!

As you look through these examples, pay particular attention to Capsules that have longer-than-normal definitions or multiple test examples. These deviations are signs that this format is adaptable to specific needs.

6

Concept Capsule Samples:
English Language Arts

DEFINE: ALLEGORY

- a story, poem, or even a picture that has a hidden meaning
- Fables are a type of allegory.
- In an allegory, a person often stands for a character trait (like honesty).
- different from a symbol in that it is an entire story, not just a single object
- from the Latin *allegoria*, meaning "veiled language" or "figurative"

This painting by the artist Titian is called *Allegory of Prudence*. The three human heads represent the three stages of human life (young, maturity, and old age). It is the three-headed beast that is the symbol of prudence. Insider tip: Titian himself is the model for the old man.

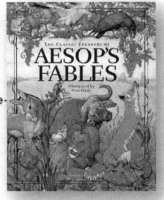

Aesop's *Fables* are some of the most famous allegories in the world. Want to read a few? Visit aesopfables.com.

What It Looks Like on A Test:

All of the following are true about allegories EXCEPT:

- A. The meanings are deeper than the surface.
- B. They are always true stories.
- C. They have a message for the reader or viewer.
- D. They use symbolism.

Unscramble the tiles to reveal a message.

Use the spaces below to write the letters in the correct order.

ALL	S .	SYM	STO	RE	S A
RIE	RIE	EGO	I C	BOL	

DEFINE: ALLITERATION

- A number of words starting with the same first consonant sound appearing in a series close together
- An example is: Pound the peanuts on the purple plate.
- Alliteration depends upon the *sound*, not the *letter*.
- Alliteration must have both the sound similarity *and* the closeness of the sequence.
- From the Latin *latira*, meaning "letters of the alphabet"

Businesses sometimes use alliteration in their names. Notice how Krispy Kreme changed the first letters of the words, even though we know it's the sound that matters, not the letter. Would you have done that? Can you think of any others in addition to these?

Ed Heck's book *Many Marvelous Monsters* is chock full of alliteration.

What It Looks Like on A Test:

In this excerpt from Shakespeare's play *Romeo and Juliet*, underline the examples of alliteration (hint: there are two different sounds and six words involved).

"From forth the fatal loins of these two foes; A pair of star-cross'd lovers take their life."

Take the first consonant of your first name and create a sentence with at least five alliterative words in it that begin with that consonant.

Example: If your name were Ethan, the letter would be "t." A possible sentence could be: Ten traveling truck drivers trundled down the road terribly.

Your sentence:

_____

_____

DEFINE: ANTAGONIST

- A character who opposes the protagonist
- A person or organization hostile to another person, group, or idea
- An adversary or enemy, but not necessarily a bad person or thing
- Originally, it was just used in sports, but about 1620 it extended to anything.

Lord Voldemort is one of the most famous antagonists in literature. Can you think of one who is worse?

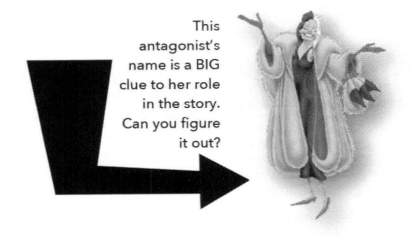

This antagonist's name is a BIG clue to her role in the story. Can you figure it out?

What It Looks Like on A Test:

What is the role of the antagonist in this story?

    A. The antagonist makes the characters hate each other.
    B. The protagonists are happier because of him.
    C. He makes their mother abandon them.
    D. He reveals the weakness in some of their plans.

Draw lines from the antagonists to the things they oppose.

Antagonists	What Is Opposed
Wizard	Goldilocks
boredom	targets
bullies	happiness
Three Bears	Cinderella
wicked stepmother	Dorothy
Shere Khan	Mowgli

DEFINE: IRONY

- when there is a contrast between expectation and reality
- comes in three kinds: verbal, situational, and dramatic
- In dramatic irony, the audience knows something the characters don't know.
- from the French "ironie", and before that, the Latin "ironia"

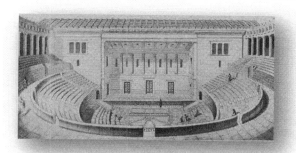

In ancient Greek drama, there was a stock character known as *Eiron*. An Eiron character pretends his abilities are lower than they are so he can defeat his opponent. Saying less than you mean is a type of irony.

Want to learn more about verbal irony? You can watch this video https://bit.ly/verb-irony (see if you agree with the criticism of the video in the comments!).

What It Looks Like on A Test:

Label the following either verbal (v), situational (s), or dramatic (d) irony or not an example of irony (n):

The reader knows the character is walking into a trap, but the character doesn't know. ___
Saying "I think this tastes great," when you don't really like it. ___
Going to the store even if you don't want to. ___
Working for ten years to pay off an expensive necklace you lost and then finding out that the necklace was fake. ___

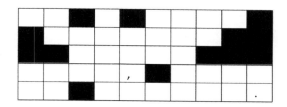

Solve Me!

If you need instructions for solving a fallen phrase puzzle, you can watch this video: https://bit.ly/fallen-phrase.

DEFINE: METAPHOR

- A metaphor says that one thing actually *is* another thing or is a substitute for that thing, when it actually is not that thing.
- A metaphor uses "is" or "are" or "was" or "were", not "like" or "as."
- For example, "My love is a red, red rose" is a metaphor. Your love is not *actually* a red rose.
- Like a simile, a metaphor allows the writer or speaker to make a word picture.
- Metaphor: love **IS** a red, red, rose; Simile: love is **LIKE** a red, red rose
- From a Greek word that means to transfer or to carry over

By Mark Teague

If you think your bedroom is a pigsty this book is for you. It's all about a kid who finds actual pigs in his room – and they fit right in!

This entire (very short) poem is a metaphor.

Hope is the thing with feathers
That perches on the soul
And sings the tune without the words
And never stops at all.

What It Looks Like on A Test:

Change this simile to a metaphor: *He is as hungry as a horse.*

OR…

Create a metaphor that compares school to something appropriate.

School is _____.

Metaphor Cryptogram! (Need help solving a cryptogram? Look here: bit.ly/solve-cryptogram)

A	B	C	D	E	F	G	H	I	J	K	L	M	N	O	P	Q	R	S	T	U	V	W	X	Y	Z
				20								21			4		1								

M	E	_	_	P	_	_	R	_		_	R	E	_	_	_	_		P	_	_	_	_	E	_
21	20	14	12	4	7	18	1	15		12	1	20	21	23	9	25		4	13	3	3	5	20	15

DEFINE: ONOMATOPOEIA

- a word that sounds like what it represents ("pow" or a stream that "gushes")
- creates a sound effect that imitates the thing it's talking about (*buzz*, *splash*, *thump*, *roar*, *meow*, *woof*, *whisper*, and on and on)
- the word comes from two Greek words: *onoma* ("name") and *poien* ("to make"). It means, "to make a name or a sound."

You'll find loads of onomatopoeia in comic books. They're chock-full of *Bam!* and *Pow!* and *Crash!* There's even a DC comic character named Onomatopoeia. Guess what kinds of words he says?

Onomatopoeia sounds different in different languages. For instance, the sound for sneezing in English, "achoo," is "achhee" in Hindi and "hatschi" in German.

What It Looks Like on A Test:

Which of the following onomatopoeic words would NOT represent the sound of a stream?
   A. gushing
   B. whispering
   C. crunching
   D. splashing

```
S P M E O W M B I X
J O C L I C K C P P
D O R T D Z O R O S
H F P A G M N U P S
J J O I N K E N P T
M D R L E J I C L K
O V V L Q C G H O N
O D M O A N H N P A
P V I Q N K I A Q L
Q X T I M B W G W C
```

Find the Onomatopoeia words!

clank	click	crunch
meow	moan	moo
neigh	oink	plop
poof	psst	?

There's one more in there! Can you find it?

DEFINE: PARADOX

- A statement that seems absurd or contradicts itself, but turns out to be true
- A statement that sounds reasonable but leads to a conclusion that doesn't make sense or contradicts itself
- A person or a thing or a situation that has contradictory qualities or features (someone who is mean and nice, or a party that is fun and boring)
- From the Greek *paradoxon* "contrary opinion"

Shakespeare loves paradox. Loves it. Here's an example from *Romeo and Juliet*:

JULIET: My only love sprung from my only hate! / Too early seen unknown, and known too late!

See it? She loves him, but her family hates his family. She knows him too early because they're so young, but it's too late because their families are already enemies.

Paradoxes aren't just in literature. They're important in philosophy as well. One super interesting paradox is called the Liar's paradox. Want to learn more? Visit brainden.com/paradoxes.htm or scan the code.

What It Looks Like on A Test:

In this paradox, what unexpected truth is the reader supposed to realize?

His greatest flaw was his greatest strength. To overcome one was to lose the other. Everyone wanted him to do the first, not knowing the result.

OR: You might also see a [much easier] question like, *"Jumbo shrimp" is an example of which literary device?*

Play with Paradox! Match the terms to create paradoxes.

wise	peace	1.
War is	more	2.
Spend to	fool	3.
Less is	save	4.

DEFINE: PERSONIFICATION

- giving non-human things human characteristics
- It can be a thing, an animal, or even an abstract idea like *truth* or *human nature*
- Personification can give human feelings, actions, or expressions (like frowning)

The ad says that Oreos® are milk's favorite cookie, but milk can't *really* have a favorite, can it? Just like goldfish crackers can't really smile back.

Carl Sandburg's poem *Fog* is short, but full of personification. Scan the code to read it. How many examples can you find?

What It Looks Like on A Test:

"All the little wood things—the ferns and the satin leaves and the crackerberries—have gone to sleep, just as if somebody had tucked them away until spring under a blanket of leaves." - *Anne of Green Gables*, L.M. Montgomery

This sentence is an example of which literary element?

    A. Simile

    B. Metaphor

    C. Personification

    D. Extended rhyme

Personify! Add in a verb that would be something a human would do.

1. Lightning _____ across the sky.
2. The wind _____ in the night.
3. My alarm _____ at me every morning.
4. The desk _____ under the weight of the books.
5. Computers get _____ when people restart them.

DEFINE: PROTAGONIST

- the leading character or one of the major characters in a play, a story, or a movie, sometimes called the "hero"
- A protagonist can be an important person in a real-life situation.
- The protagonist does not have to be a good person and often has very annoying characteristics. They're the protagonist because they drive the story's action forward.
- opposed by the antagonist
- from the Greek *protos* (first in importance) and *agonistes* (actor)

Sometimes stories have more than one protagonist. In *The Lion, the Witch and the Wardrobe,* there are four protagonists, but none of them are the character on the cover!

This popular Christmas story has a protagonist who starts out pretty evil! Do you think he stays that way?

What It Looks Like on A Test:

Which of the following is NOT true of the protagonist?

- A. The protagonist drives the story's action forward.
- B. There can be more than one of them in a story.
- C. The protagonist is only found in fiction.
- D. Characters who work against the protagonist are called the "antagonist."

Draw Lines from the Protagonists to Their Stories!

Where the Wild Things Are	A bear
I Want My Hat Back	August
The Secret Garden	Max
Wonder	Mary

DEFINE: SIMILE

- comparing two different things using words such as *like*, *as*, *than*, or a verb like *resembles*
- A simile says that two things are alike in some specific way (*as* hard *as* a rock).
- Using a simile allows the writer or speaker to make a word picture.
- Simile: love is **LIKE** a red, red rose; Metaphor: love **IS** a red, red, rose
- from the Latin *similis* "like"

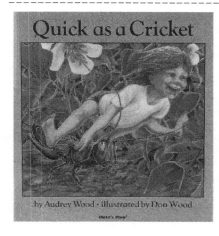

The whole book *Quick as a Cricket* is written in similes. You may have read the author's other book, *The Napping House*.

Scan this QR code to get a list of bad similes!

What It Looks Like on A Test:

What two things are being compared in this simile? What characteristic do they share?

I'm more tired than a horse after a hundred-mile ride.

OR...

Create a simile using either *like* or *than* or *resembles* that compares the sun to something that is found in the ocean.

Play with these similes!

My _____ is as hard as a rock. His shirt is brighter than _____.

The coat on the dog resembles _____. That candy is like _____.

The _____ is as sturdy as a fortress. Her _____ is like a lemon.

DEFINE: THEME

- the central idea of a story – what the story means, what it's about
- Stories can have more than one theme.
- Usually the author doesn't tell you the theme. You have to figure it out.
- The theme can often be expressed in a single word like "jealousy" or "hope."

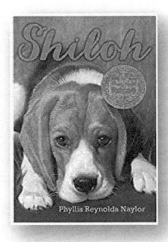

The book *Shiloh* has several themes, including the importance of friendship, responsibility, and justice. If you've read it, you can probably think of others!

Anna Geiger put together this list of children's books with the theme of friendship. many

Scan the QR code or visit this site: https://themeasuredmom.com/books-about-friendship.

What It Looks Like on A Test:

This excerpt from Rick Riordan's, *The Sea of Monsters,* supports what theme?

"Families are messy. Immortal families are eternally messy. Sometimes the best we can do is to remind each other that we're related for better or for worse…and try to keep the maiming and killing to a minimum." (from *The Sea of Monsters*)."

A. Messiness   B. Family   C. Immortality   D. Happiness

THEME IT!

Think of your last year in school. Choose a theme from the list below (or come up with one of your own) and explain why you think that is a good theme to represent the year.

PERSEVERANCE   STRUGGLE   IMPORTANCE OF WORK   RELATIONSHIPS

_____

_____

7

Concept Capsule Samples:
Math

DEFINE: ACUTE ANGLE

- an angle that measures less than 90 degrees
- always smaller than a right angle
- The range of an acute angle is between 0 and 90 degrees.
- from the Latin word for "sharp"

A slice of pizza may be the most important acute angle in the world, although the builders of the pyramids (full of acute angles) may disagree!

Can you think of any other foods with cute little angles? I mean, acute angles?

Pro Tip: The letter "A" has an acute angle. Do you see it?

What It Looks Like on A Test:

Which of the following is NOT an acute angle?

A. 93 degrees
B. 45 degrees
C. 32 degrees
D. 78 degrees

OR

Draw an acute angle.

Which of these clocks has/have an acute angle?

Now draw your own acute angle here!

DEFINE: ANGLE

- a shape formed by two rays sharing a common point (the vertex)
- the amount of turn between two lines around their common point
- measured in degrees with a protractor in a counter-clockwise direction
- from the Latin *angulus,* meaning "corner." In Latin, the root *ang-* means to bend. The form we see it in literally means "a little bend."

Clocks are an everyday example of angles. See how the hands of the clock are the rays? In an angle, the rays are called the "sides" of the angle.

Cool fact: Angle is also a verb that means "to fish." That's because the root word shares the idea of bending something into a hook. Someone who fishes is called an "angler."

What It Looks Like on A Test:

Why would you MOST LIKELY use a protractor?

- A. to measure straight lines
- B. to determine if something is positive or negative
- C. to tell the temperature
- D. to measure angles
- E. to draw a straight line

Besides clocks, there are lots of examples of angles all around you!

Look around and see how many you can find!

_____   _____   _____

_____   _____   _____

_____   _____   _____

DEFINE: COMPOSITE NUMBER

- whole numbers with more than two factors
- whole numbers that are not prime because they are divisible by more than one number
- positive integer formed by multiplying two other positive integers

Mount Fuji

Volcanoes that are formed from lots of layers of lava, pumice, ash, and tephra (instead of lava) are called composite volcanoes (or stratovolcanoes). Do you see the connection between them and composite numbers?

Fun Fact: Composite numbers that are formed from multiplying three distinct prime numbers are called "sphenic numbers." The smallest sphenic number is 30. It's the product of the three smallest prime numbers. What are they?

30

42

66

What It Looks Like on A Test:

Which of these numbers is a composite number?

A. 17
B. 23
C. 36
D. 51

Solve the Composite Puzzle!

				18
2				20
4	8			21
		4	2	20
			6	25
19	24	19	24	20

The missing numbers are integers between 0 and 9.

The numbers in each row add up totals to the right.

The number in each column add up to the totals along the bottom.

The diagonal lines also add up the totals to the right.

Solve the puzzle & circle all the composite numbers.

DEFINE: DIAMETER

- segment whose endpoints lie on the circle and whose midpoint is the center of the circle
- the largest distance from one side of a circle to the other side
- from the Greek *diametros* meaning "line measuring across"; from *dia-* meaning "across" + *metron-* meaning "measure."

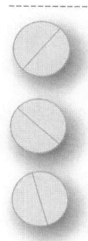

All of these images show the diameter of the circle. It doesn't matter from which point on the circle you start – as long as it goes through the center of the circle and is a straight line from one side to the other, it's a diameter. There are an infinite number of possible diameters on a circle.

Let's talk about something really important: cookies. If I want to split this cookie exactly in half, I will cut it on a diameter. It doesn't matter where I start on the edge of the circle, as long as I cut across the circle going through the middle, I'll have cut it in half.

What It Looks Like on A Test:

Your teacher is trying to convince you that this is the diameter of the circle. Explain why your teacher is wrong and how you know.

Find the Biggest Diameter!

Grab a ruler and go find at least five items in your house that have circles (it could be a picture of a circle on something or the top/bottom of a glass or bowl). Measure those diameters. What were they? Which item had the largest diameter?

1. _____   5. _____
2. _____   6. _____
3. _____   7. _____
4. _____   The winner is: _____

DEFINE: DIVIDEND

- the amount or number that is to be divided
- the number inside the long division symbol ➡)‾‾‾‾‾
- dividend = divisor x quotient + remainder
- also the amount of money paid by a company to its shareholders

The word "divide" is from the Latin *dividere*, which means "to force apart."

To help you remember which number in a division problem is the dividend, think about which number is being forced apart. In the case of these puppies, the dividend is the rope!

Watch and listen to this division story *The Doorbell Rang*.

https://bit.ly/doorbell-rang.

The Doorbell Rang By Pat Hutchins : Children's Book Read Aloud

---

What It Looks Like on A Test:

The divisor in an equation is 10. The quotient is 5. There is no remainder. What is the dividend?

A. 15
B. 25
C. 30
D. 50

It Needs a Name!

We've been using the long division symbol since 1888, but it still has no name!

Ask at least five people what they think it should be called and use tally marks to track their votes.

There are four possibilities listed here. Feel free to add options of your own. What was the winning name?

)‾‾‾‾‾‾‾‾

Option 1: division table

Option 2: dividend tent

Option 3: division bracket

Option 4: division house

Other:

DEFINE: HISTOGRAM

- a graph that groups data into ranges (called "bins widths") and displays those bin widths as rectangles/bars called "bins"
- the area of the bar shows how many items are in each data range
- usually has the independent variable plotted along the horizontal axis and the dependent variable plotted along the vertical axis.

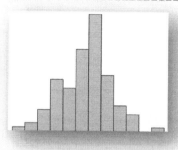

Don't Be Fooled! Some people confuse histograms and bar graphs. Histograms are different from a bar graph because they are numerical (bar graphs can have categories) and the bars touch (in bar graphs, the bars shouldn't touch). See those touchy bars? Yep, histogram. Now you're a pro!

If you'd like a review on how to create a histogram, this video will show you how! https://bit.ly/histogram-howto

What It Looks Like on A Test:

Identify the type of graph this is.

_____

Based on this representation, is it accurate to say that more dogs weigh between 11-15kg than weight between 16-20kg?

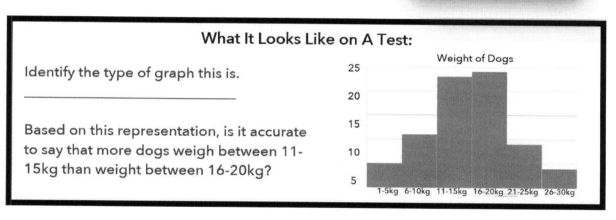

Weight of Dogs

In the game Scrabble®, "histogram" is a 15-point word! That's quite a word!

How many words can you make out of the word "histogram"?

DEFINE: IMPROPER FRACTION

- a fraction where the numerator (the top number) is greater than or equal to the denominator (the bottom number).
- always 1 or greater than 1 (proper fractions are always greater than zero, but less than 1).
- can be converted to mixed fraction (with a whole number and a fraction)

"Improper" doesn't have anything to do with manners in math! You will see it in proper functions and proper subsets, too.

Fun Fact: The term "improper fraction" was first used in 1542 by Welsh doctor and mathematician Robert Recorde in the first English book on Algebra, *The Ground of artes, teachyng the worke and practise of arithmetike.* (You can see that proper spelling wasn't a thing in the 16th century!) He also invented the equals sign!

What It Looks Like on A Test:
Identify the improper fractions and convert them to proper fractions.

$$\frac{5}{5} \qquad \frac{8}{6} \qquad \frac{2}{5} \qquad \frac{9}{10} \qquad \frac{6}{6} \qquad \frac{5}{3}$$

Improper Fractions as Easy as Pie!

Devonte brought delicious blackberry pie that his dad made to a party. There was so much pie! Yummy, yummy pie!

He cut the pies into six pieces, like this.

Javier ate an entire pie, plus three more pieces. He was hungry!

Because the pie was cut into six pieces, we can say that Javier ate $\frac{9}{6}$ of a pie!

DEFINE: ISOSCELES TRIANGLE

- triangle with two equal (congruent) sides
- has two equal (congruent) angles
- from the Greek *iso-* meaning "same" + *skelos* meaning "leg" (makes sense because the two equal sides are called the "legs"); in early English called *tweyleke* (two like)

The famous Flatiron Building in New York city is an isosceles triangle. It got its name because it looks like a clothes iron. It's one of the most famous buildings in New York, probably because math is just that cool.

Euclid said an isosceles triangle could only have TWO equal sides, but now we usually let equilateral triangles (3 equal sides) in the club, too. What do you think?

What It Looks Like on A Test:

Remembering that the sum of the angles of a triangle is 180 degrees...If an isosceles triangle has two angles measuring 73 degrees, what is the measure of the vertex angle?

A. 117
B. 43
C. 28
D. 34

The Secret Code of Triangles

See those lines on the legs of this cool isosceles triangle? They are a secret math code that means, "We're the same." That way, you don't have to measure them to check. You can tell because you're in the know. You're like a math secret agent.

See those quarter circles on the angles at the bottom? Yep, same. They are the secret code that says, "We're the same."

Don't feel badly for that angle that looks left out. It gets its own name: the vertex angle.

DEFINE: MEAN

- the average you arrive at when you add up all of the numbers in a set and then divide by the number of numbers in the set
- the central value in a set of numbers
- also called the arithmetic mean, the average, or the expected value
- shown by symbol $\bar{x}$, pronounced "x bar"

Beware of the average!

Averages can be misleading if you're using them to think about what something is really like. For instance, NASA says the average temperature of the Earth is 15°C (59°F). How many days a year is that really the temperature where you live? You've been warned: "average" is not the same as "always."

There are three kinds of averages: mean, median, and mode. You can learn how to calculate them all in this song: https://bit.ly/median-song

3M's - Mean, Median and Mode Rap | Mister C (Song #7)

What It Looks Like on A Test:

Calculate the mean of this data set: 32, 15, 47, 27, 9, 50.

The $\bar{x}$ of the set is: _____.

You're the Mathematician!

Collect at least seven data points from people you know and calculate their mean. You can choose any data set you want. Here are examples: peoples' heights, number of states people have visited, number of siblings people have, number of pets people have, how many pairs of shoes do they own.

Record the data points:

Calculate the mean:

DEFINE: MODE

- the most frequent number in a data set
- the item that occurs the highest number of times in a data set
- To find the mode, put the numbers in order. Count how many of each number occurs in the data set. The one appearing most often is the mode.
- If no number is repeated, the set of numbers has no mode. A set can also have more than one mode.
- also called the modal value

Mode is cool because it's the measure of average that can use non-numbers in the set. You can have a mode in a set of colors, places, names, or just about any set of data! For example, if in a classroom of 25 students, 6 are wearing blue shirts, 3 are wearing red shirts, 1 is wearing a yellow shirt, and 11 are wearing green shirts, green is the mode of the set.

Mathematician Karl Pearson is the person who first called it "mode." It's not surprising because he is the one who established the discipline of mathematical statistics.

What It Looks Like on A Test:

Determine if this set has zero, one, or two modes: blue, blue, green, yellow, red, orange, yellow, purple, red, red, blue, green, blue

This set has (circle)   zero   one   two   mode(s).

Fill in the Blank

The mode is the most _____ number in a data set. That's one way to remember it: it's the one that show up mo_____. A data set can have more than one _____ or even _____ mode. Modes are cool because they work for things other than _____. To find the mode, put the numbers (or other data) in order. Then _____ how many times each thing appears in the set.

DEFINE: OBTUSE ANGLE

- an angle that measures more than 90 degrees and less than 180 degrees
- always larger than a right angle
- from the Latin word for "dull" or "blunt"

The kind of fan you hold in your hand and flick open forms an obtuse angle when it's fully open.

Pro Tip: The letter "Y" has an obtuse angle. Do you see it? Actually, you should see *them,* because there are two, one on each side!
The letters X and K have obtuse angles, too. One of those letters has two obtuse angles, and one only has one. Can you figure out which is which?

Y

What It Looks Like on A Test:

Describe this angle and use the correct term to identify it.

OR

Draw an obtuse angle.

Obtuse angles are all around us!

Go to your kitchen or bathroom and open a cupboard door all of the way. Boom! Obtuse angle!

Now go find a book or notebook. Open it up until it's lying like this. Since books can't open all the way to 180 degrees, you've got an obtuse angle!

Can you find another one in your house? Hint: go outside & look up!

DEFINE: PERIMETER

- the distance around a two-dimensional shape
- the sum of the length of all of the sides of a polygon
- when applying to a circle, usually called the circumference

This is the Pentagon building in Washington, D.C. It is a true pentagon. Each side is 921 feet in length, giving it a perimeter of 4,605 feet.

The country with the largest perimeter in the world is (drumroll, please) Canada! It has a perimeter of 146,000km! Whew!

This video has a strong discussion of what perimeter is, along with instructions for how to find the perimeter of polygons! Super fun! https://bit.ly/perimeter-howto

Math Antics - Perimeter

What It Looks Like on A Test:

What do you need to know to find the perimeter of this polygon?

Assuming all lines are parallel or perpendicular, do you have enough information to figure it out yourself? Why or why not?

20cm
16cm
6cm
2cm
4cm
18cm
2cm

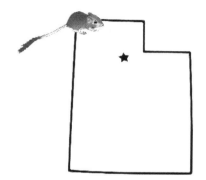

Help a Rat Out!

This kangaroo rat is considering moving to this state (any guesses which state it is?). She decides to try to find out how far around this state really is. How would you explain to her how to find the answer to what she's looking for and what mathematicians would call it?

8

Concept Capsule Samples: Science

DEFINE: ABSORB

- to take something up or in; to soak up liquid in the process called absorption
- in biology – passing of nutrient material/chemicals into tissue, such as through the blood or the walls of the intestine
- in physics – taking in radiant energy (as opposed to reflecting it) or the partial loss of energy (light, radio waves, etc.), as it passes through something
- from the Latin *absorbere*, *ab-* (from) + *sorbere* (suck in)

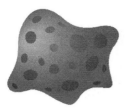

To be able to absorb liquid, a substance has to have space to store the liquid molecules. No space = no absorption. Some substances, like sponge or paper, attract water molecules. The super cool word for this is *hygroscopy*. If something is hygroscopic, it attracts water. Honey is hygroscopic. Isn't that cool? #wordlove

Light and sound waves can also be absorbed when they encounter matter. If the wave is absorbed, it transfers its energy to the material it is going through. The molecules of the material start vibrating from the energy, producing heat. That's why sand burns your feet! Some of the energy of the Sun's electromagnetic waves is absorbed by the sand. Ouch!

What It Looks Like on A Test:

If you needed to wipe up a cup of spilled water, you would need the material you were wiping it up with to be able to:

    A. repel the water
    B. absorb the water
    C. evaporate the water
    D. reflect the water

OR

Explain why some materials absorb water & others don't.

If someone says that sand is moving, explain why that person is correct.

Help out this scientist! She is studying absorption and can't decide which materials are most likely to absorb water. Circle the ones you think she should choose.

paper	aluminum foil	soil
steel	plastic	sponge
cotton	wax paper	fabric

DEFINE: ADAPTATION

- when animals become better matched to their environment to help them survive or thrive
- can be a body part, body covering, or a behavior
- can be general (walking or flying or swimming) or specific (webbed feet, sharp claws, long beaks)
- happens over long periods of slow change

The puffer fish (also called a blowfish) fills its stomach with air to expand to about twice its normal size when it feels threatened.

The octopus has an astonishing ability to camouflage itself. Watch this video compilation of it in action! https://bit.ly/octo-change

---

What It Looks Like on A Test:

Why would animals engage in this behavioral adaptation?

    A. to find food or water
    B. to find better living conditions
    C. to stay within a country's boundaries
    D. 1 & 2
    E. 1 & 3

The toucan has developed a very large beak that lets it reach fruit on light branches. They can even adjust the flow of blood to their beak! At night, they tuck their beak under their wings to keep warm. Sketch out a toucan and color in their beak in the color you think it should be!

DEFINE: ANIMAL POPULATION

- number of individuals of a particular species living in an area that can breed with each other
- can be more than one population in an area
- impacted by limiting factors like food, water, and shelter

Some animal populations are easy to count, like elephants. Can you think of an animal population that would be harder to count?

 If you're interested in the populations of certain animals, you can find great data at
http://systemanaturae.org/datasets

What It Looks Like on A Test:

This chart supports which of the following statements about animal population in Africa?

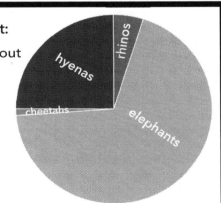

A. All of the populations are about the same.
B. The population of hyenas is greater than the population of elephants.
C. The population of rhinos is growing.
D. There are more rhinos than cheetahs.

Count the population! Imagine that you are a population biologist studying humans in your area. Research the population of humans in the following areas:

Population of humans in your home	
Population of humans in your school	
Population of humans in your town	
Population of humans in your state	
Population of humans in your country	
Population of humans on your planet	

Which population(s) is/are growing? Which are not? Are there any other animal populations in your home or school besides humans?

DEFINE: ARID

- climate that is extremely dry, with very little precipitation
- a place without enough rain to support plant life
- also called "xeric"
- from Latin *arere*, meaning "to be dry or parched"

One of the coolest desert plants is the Saguaro cactus. It's found only in the Sonoran Desert. A saguaro can live to be 150 to 200 years old and grown 60 feet tall! It's pronounced suh- waa- row.

More than a third of the world is an arid climate. Most arid climates are found 30 degrees north or south of the equator because of the Earth's wind patterns. That means the Earth has a big arid belt!

What It Looks Like on A Test:

Describe the challenge of growing wheat in an arid climate.

OR

The lack of which of the following is the most important factor in an arid climate?
- A. heat
- B. light
- C. soil
- D. rain

Sketch out an arid climate. Include at least three kinds of cactus in your sketch.

DEFINE: BIOME

- a specific geographic area notable for the species of plants and animals living there
- plants and animals in the biome adapt to thrive in the biome
- A biome will often have many different ecosystems within it.
- Abiotic factors like climate and habitat are part of the biome as well.
- The number of biomes identified varies all the way from 5 to 20.

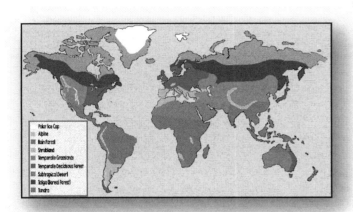

When you're looking at a biome map, you don't care about country borders. You only care about the area of the biome. The maps will look different depending upon how many biomes are identified on the map.

Explore biomes with this cool interactive biome globe! You can put a pin anywhere on the globe, and it will tell you all about the climate, plants, and animals living there: https://bit.ly/biome-map.

What It Looks Like on A Test:

Describe why plant and animal diversity in a biome is limited.
OR
Determine if each of these statements is true or false:
1. There can be different names for the same biome. _____
2. Biomes are all the same size. _____
3. Biomes have different levels of plant and animal diversity. _____

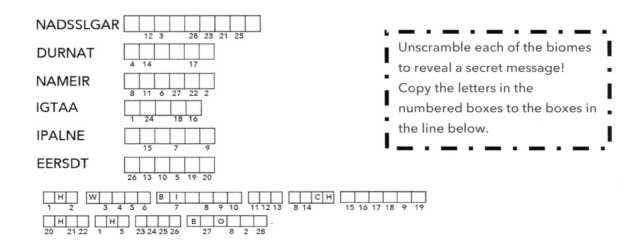

NADSSLGAR [ ][ ][ ][ ][ ][ ][ ][ ]
         12 3   28 23 21 25

DURNAT [ ][ ][ ][ ][ ][ ]
     4 14   17

NAMEIR [ ][ ][ ][ ][ ][ ]
   8 11 6 27 22 2

IGTAA [ ][ ][ ][ ][ ]
   1 24 18 16

IPALNE [ ][ ][ ][ ][ ][ ]
    15   7   9

EERSDT [ ][ ][ ][ ][ ][ ]
  26 13 10 5 19 20

Unscramble each of the biomes to reveal a secret message! Copy the letters in the numbered boxes to the boxes in the line below.

[ ][H][ ][W][ ][ ][ ][ ][B][I][ ][ ][ ][ ][ ][ ][ ][C][H][ ][ ][ ][ ][ ][ ][ ]
1 2   3 4 5 6   7   8 9 10 11 12 13 8 14   15 16 17 18 9 19

[ ][H][ ][ ][H][ ][ ][ ][ ][B][ ][O][ ][ ][ ] .
20 21 22 1   5 23 24 25 26   27 8 2 28

DEFINE: CHEMICAL CHANGE

- chemical reaction that produces one or more new substances
- The arrangement of the atoms in the molecules is what changes; the atoms are the same.
- different from a physical change in that the substance itself changes, not just the physical properties of the substance (changes what it is, not just how it looks)
- You can tell that there's been a chemical reaction because the substance will release or absorb heat (or other energy), or produce a gas, odor, color or sound.

Fireworks are one of the coolest examples of chemical change. An apple turning brown may not be as much fun, but it's an example, too.

Watch this video about chemical change to learn more. What lab safety issues would you discuss with him? https://bit.ly/change-chem

What It Looks Like on A Test:

Identify the following as a chemical change or a physical change. If it is a physical change, name something you could do to make create a chemical change.

1. Stirring up cake batter _____
2. Cooking an egg _____
3. Ripping up a piece of paper _____
4. The underside of a car rusting out _____

Fill in the blanks to make this passage accurate and complete.

When green bananas turn yellow, that is an example of _____ change even though they are still bananas. If you crumple a piece of paper, that's a _____ change. If you burn that paper, that is an example of a _____ change because you traded paper for heat, light and ash. One sign it's a chemical reaction is that it produced _____ or _____ or _____ or _____.

DEFINE: CLOSED CIRCUIT

- complete loop around which electricity can flow
- must have a source of electricity (such as a battery or power outlet) and a conductor (like wire)
- the load of a circuit is what consumes electrical power
- from the Latin *circuitus*, *circum-* (around) + *ire* (go), so literally "go around"

The *load* in a circuit is the work the electricity has to do. A light bulb is an example of load in an electrical circuit. It's what uses the electricity. In your house, appliances like toasters and refrigerators are the most common examples of load.

Want to learn more about circuits? Watch this video: https://bit.ly/learn-circuits.

The Power of Circuits #sciencegoals

What It Looks Like on A Test:

Label this drawing of a closed circuit:

What could you do to make this an open circuit?

_____

_____

_____

Choose Your Source!

Circle the two sources of electricity. Which one would you choose if you needed to power a dishwasher?

_____

DEFINE: CONDENSATION

- process by which water vapor in the air is changed into liquid water
- one of four main stages of the water cycle
- opposite of evaporation
- essential because it makes precipitation possible

Clouds are formed when warm, moist air cools. The water vapor condenses on tiny particles in the air, forming tiny water droplets that are what make up clouds!

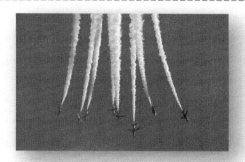

Airplane contrails (condensation trails!) are example of condensation you may have noticed. They are created when water vapor in the jet exhaust condenses on tiny particles in the air.

What It Looks Like on A Test:

What evidence of condensation is shown in this image?

A. rain
B. ground
C. clouds
D. A &C

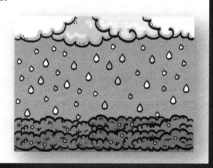

Find all these condensation words!

```
I X R A G M N S B O
I D P I M O H D C K
V R E O T V Y D L M
O O Z E F I L D O O
J P V L D M I R U U
P L A C H Q Q E D B
Y E P Y G I U T O A
W T O C Q H I A C B
C C R C M P D W Z C
Y L S T B P G X Q M
```

- cloud
- liquid
- water
- droplet
- vapor
- cycle

DEFINE: CONDUCTIVITY

- Conductivity is the measure how easily an electric charge, sound or heat can pass through a material.
- They flow easily through materials with high conductivity.
- A conductor is a material that provides a path through which energy can flow.
- Conductivity is one of the physical properties of matter.
- Conductivity is measured in siemens per meter and is often represented using the Greek letter σ.

It sounds strange, but sound travels fastest through solids, not liquids or gases. See what we did there? *Sounds* strange? Molecules in solids are closer together than in liquids or gases, so sound transfers more quickly. It's weird, but true: sound passes through steel 17 times faster than it does through air.

The metal that is the best conductor of electricity and heat is silver. To be a good conductor, electricity or heat passing through it has to be able to move the electrons of the material. The more free electrons a substance has, the greater its conductivity. Silver is loaded with free electrons, making it conductivity metal #1!

What It Looks Like on A Test:

Which of the following statements is MOST complete AND most true?
   A. Conductivity measures how easily energy flows through a substance.
   B. Materials with high conductivity allow electricity to flow through them with only mild difficulty.
   C. A conductor allows an electric charge or heat to flow through it, but it doesn't

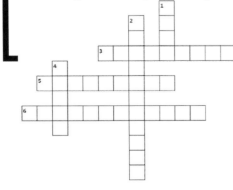

Across

3. Lots of free _____ make for good conductivity
5. A resource that provides a path for energy to flow.
6. A physical property of matter that describes how well electricity, heat, and sound flow through a substance.

Down
1. This flows easily through good conductors.
2. This flows easily through good conductors.
4. This flows easily through good conductors.

DEFINE: CONSUMER

- organisms in a food chain that get their energy by eating other organisms
- primary consumers eat plants (also called herbivores)
- secondary consumers eat primary consumers (also called carnivores)
- tertiary consumers eat secondary consumers (can be carnivores [meat eaters] or omnivores [eat plants and animals])
- fancy word for consumer: heterotroph

Koalas are a type of primary consumer called *specialists*. That means they eat only one food (or strongly prefers one food). For koalas, it's eucalyptus. Specialists are more vulnerable because if their preferred food becomes unavailable, they don't adapt well.

Some food chains even have a fourth level of consumer, called a quaternary consumer. The shark is a quaternary consumer in this food chain: phytoplankton – zooplankton – fish- seal – shark.

What It Looks Like on A Test:

A grasshopper eats grass. It is then eaten by a rat. The rat would be happy to eat other foods, too. The rat is eaten by a snake. Which of the following statements is accurate?

A. The grasshopper is a primary consumer & the snake is a secondary consumer.

B. The rat is a primary consumer and a specialist.

C. The rat is a secondary consumer and a specialist.

D. The rat is a tertiary consumer and the snake is a quaternary consumer.

E. The grasshopper is not a consumer.

How many consumers can you find in this food chain? Label them as primary, secondary or tertiary consumers!

DEFINE: CORE

- the very hot center of our planet
- made of metals (mostly iron and nickel)
- made of two parts, a solid inner core and a spinning molten outer core
- inner core's temperature equal to that of the Sun; outer core's temperature slightly cooler

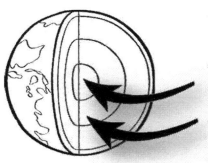

The core of the Earth is exactly where you'd expect to find it!

Just like the core of an apple, it's in the middle!

Danish scientist Inge Lehmann discovered that the core of the Earth was solid in 1936.

Before her, scientists believed that both the inner and outer cores were liquid.

What It Looks Like on A Test:

Which of the following BEST describes the inner core of the Earth?
- A. the outside layer of the Earth that is the core of what it means to be the Earth
- B. the very hot, solid center of the Earth made of iron and nickel
- C. layer of the Earth sometimes called the lithosphere
- D. the spinning molten layer at the center of the Earth
- E. none of the above

Across:

3. the inner core is this, not molten

4. one of the metals that makes up the core

5. the scientist who discovered the nature of the inner core

7. the outer core is this, not solid

Down:

1. one of the metals that makes up the core

2. the center of the Earth

3. the outer core does this

6. the core is this, not tepid

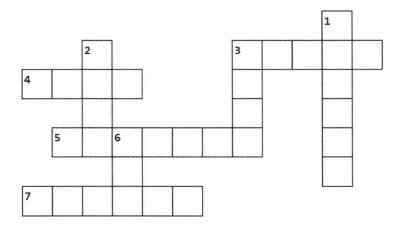

9

Concept Capsule Samples: Social Studies

DEFINE: ABSOLUTE LOCATION

- describes the location of a place based on a fixed point, usually latitude and longitude
- Every place on the Earth has a single absolute location.
- Absolution location is one of two kinds of location (along with relative location).

The happiest place on Earth is located at:

33° 48' 45'' N

117° 55' 8'' W

What do you think it is?

The castle there was inspired by this castle, located at 47° 33' 27'' N 10° 44' 58'' E.

Which of the following would be helpful in determining absolute location?

A. Latitude
B. Distance from capital city
C. Longitude
D. Name of the country
E. A & C

WHERE ARE YOU?

Put your address (or the address of the school) into the box at https://www.gps-coordinates.net. What is the coordinate (include degrees, minutes, and seconds)?

Latitude: _____ _____' _____''
Longitude: _____ _____' _____''

DEFINE: COMPASS ROSE

- a circle to display the cardinal directions (N, S, E, W) and their intermediate points on a map or chart
- sometimes called a windrose or Rose of the Winds
- gets its name from how the points on the compass resemble a rose
- can have between 4 and 32 points

- -

This enormous 8-point compass rose is so big the people sitting around it look tiny!

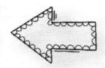

Cool fact: In the Middle Ages, the names of the winds were known by these traditional names: tramontana (N), greco (NE), levante (E), siroco (SE), ostro (S), libeccio (SW), ponente (W) and maestro (NW).

What It Looks Like on A Test:

Which of the following shows the initials of the cardinal directions around the compass rose?

A. Never Eat Soggy Waffles
B. Share Nice Eggs Wisely
C. Exciting News Shouldn't Wait
D. Would Necklaces Shine Easily?

Label the compass points on this compass rose. Do the cardinal directions first, and then the intercardinal directions. Can you figure out the names of the ones not in the chart but are on the rose?

Compass Point	Abbr.	Heading
North	N	0°
North-East	NE	45°
East	E	90°
South-East	SE	135°
South	S	180°
South-West	SW	225°
West	W	270°
North-West	NW	315°

DEFINE: CULTURE

- the way of life of a group of people
- includes language, celebrations, religion, customs, dress, food, race, traditions, philosophy, governance, and technology
- from the Latin *colere,* meaning "to tend, guard; to till, cultivate"

Many cultures have traditional dress that is used in celebrations and ceremonies. Some is simple and some is elaborate, like in this picture of a celebration in Indonesia.

There are about 6,500 languages in the world. They're divided into language families. English is part of the Indo-European language family. So are Hindi, Russian, and Spanish, but not Hungarian!

What It Looks Like on A Test:

List at least four examples of your culture. Which of those things is most important to you?

1. _____
2. _____
3. _____
4. _____

```
E C U L T U R R T E E I S I D
M G P O R T E A R C N T T R O
E C A R P L E O A N P L E E N
G T S U I D Y O D A X S C R S
S A A G G M G G I N S J U M F
N I I F E N K N T R X T A Z Z
P O O K E O A R I E J A C D Y
N O R C K J W L O V N N E E P
D N T T Y I B E N O Z P L P H
F A B T P Y H H P G H L M L X
I X B P U D O Q I U Z L Z U I
C E L E B R A T I O N S O M A
V U Q B M U A I V N S L W N S
T K W B C Q R N B S X S C Y F
Y H A E T C L U M I K C I S R
```

If you find all of these words in the puzzle, you may find a hidden message in the first three lines!

CELEBRATIONS   DRESS
RACE   FOOD
GOVERNANCE   LANGUAGE
RELIGION   TRADITION

Did you find the message?

_____

_____

DEFINE: DELTA

- low, watery land formed at the mouth of a river
- formed from the silt, sand and small rocks that flow downstream in the river and are deposited in the delta
- often (but not always) shaped like a triangle (hence its name, delta, a Greek letter Δ that is shaped like a triangle)

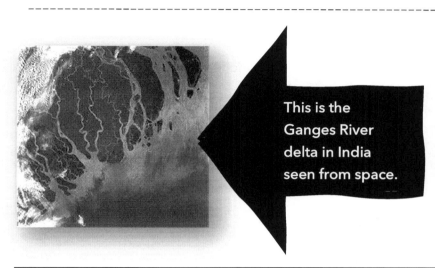

This is the Ganges River delta in India seen from space.

Read about deltas' role in history here: https://bit.ly/deltahistory or scan the code below:

What It Looks Like on A Test:

Looking at the picture shown here, which clue is NOT helpful in determining if this is a delta?

- A. It's formed by a river.
- B. It is shaped like a triangle.
- C. The river is small.
- D. There is silt build up visible where the land meets the river.

DELAT ⬚⬚⬚⬚⬚
      5 7 9

SITL ⬚⬚⬚⬚
    1

GALIRTEN ⬚⬚⬚⬚⬚⬚⬚⬚
     3   4

RREVI ⬚⬚⬚⬚⬚
    6

SEPDTSIO ⬚⬚⬚⬚⬚⬚⬚⬚
   2   10

HUTMO ⬚⬚⬚⬚⬚
    8

⬚ ⬚⬚⬚⬚ ⬚⬚⬚⬚⬚⬚
1 2 3 4 5 6 7 8 9 10

Play with Deltas!

Directions:

Unscramble each of the clue words about deltas.

Copy the letters in the numbered cells to other cells with the same number.

You'll find the secret message!

DEFINE: DEMOCRACY

- Political system in which
  - Citizens enjoy basic civil and political rights
  - Most important political leaders are elected in free and fair elections
  - Leaders are accountable under a rule of law
- From the Greek word *dēmokratia*: *demos,* meaning 'the people' + *kratia* meaning 'power or rule'

Voting is one of the most cherished aspects of any democracy.

Interested in the oldest democracies in the world? You can find more at https://bit.ly/olddemocracy or scan the code.

What It Looks Like on A Test:

If you live in a democracy, something you **wouldn't** expect would be:

A. Being allowed to vote in free and fair elections.
B. Being led by someone who didn't feel accountable to the people.
C. Basic civil rights held by all of the people.
D. All of the above.

There are 8 democracies in this wordsearch. Can you find them? If you need hints, look at the link to old democracies above.

```
I T A L Y V R D E T
X G G G F K I W F P
C N X I X C S P D S
C A N A D A R A N A
J H X H Q L A I A S
Y E F A K F E R L U
J P R O Y Y L T E B
F R A N C E J S R W
G T H U X O D U I Q
I N D I A D Y A R K
```

1.	
2.	
3.	
4.	
5.	
6.	
7.	
8.	

DEFINE: GLACIER

- dense ice that is constantly moving very slowly
- forms when snow falls faster than it can melt over many years and the weight of the snow compresses it into ice
- picks up rocks and other debris as they move, so can look dirty
- form only on land, and can create ice shelves when they reach the sea
- drastically shape the land they move over

The Mendenhall Glacier is part of the Juneau Ice Field in Alaska. It's over 13 miles long. It is currently in retreat, meaning it is melting faster than new snow is falling.

Because glaciers move so slowly, when something moves really slowly we say it's moving at a "glacial" pace. Like sloths.

What It Looks Like on A Test:

Which of the following is not true of glaciers?

A. They move slowly over the land and can form ice shelves when they reach the sea.
B. They are made of pure snow, so they are pure white.
C. As they pass over the land, they drastically shape it.
D. They store a large amount of the world's fresh water.

Glacial Trivia: Glaciers are cool. Put a star next to the fact you think is coolest.

⇒ There are about 100,000 glaciers in Alaska alone.
⇒ Nearly ¾ of the world's freshwater is stored in glaciers.
⇒ During the peak of the last ice age, about 1/3 of the Earth was covered with glaciers.
⇒ Blue is the only color of light that can penetrate (or get through) the ice, so glaciers sometimes look blue.
⇒ Scientists now think that Mars may have once had glaciers.

DEFINE: LATITUDE

- Latitude lines run east and west, circling the Earth like a stack of belts.
- Latitude is measured in degrees.
- There are 180 degrees of latitude (90 north and 90 south), and each degree is about 69 miles.
- Lines of latitude are also called parallels.
- The equator is zero degrees, and latitude describes if a place is north or south of the equator.

To help you remember which lines are latitude, think of them as a LADDER climbing the Earth.

The equator runs through 13 countries, including the beautiful country of Kenya.

What It Looks Like on A Test:

All of the following are true of latitude EXCEPT:
- A. It's measured in degrees.
- B. Lines of latitude are also called circumferences.
- C. It describes if a location is north or south of the equator.
- D. Latitude lines run east and west.

OR

Explain the difference between latitude and longitude to someone who has never heard of them.

Fill in the missing words in this passage about latitude.

Latitude is how we measure how far _____ or _____ a place is from equator. Latitude is measured in _____. The _____ is zero degrees of latitude. Latitude lines are imaginary lines circling the globe running _____ and _____.

DEFINE: LONGITUDE

- Longitude lines run north and south.
- Longitude lines are also called meridians.
- The Prime Meridian is zero degrees longitude.
- Lines of longitude place locations east or west of the Prime Meridian.
- Longitude is measured in degrees, and there are 180 degrees east and 180 degrees west of the Prime Meridian.

The Prime Meridian runs through the town of Greenwich. If you visit the Royal Observatory, you'll see this sculpture that recognizes that it is, in some ways, the center of the world. (photo by Panarimo)

This guy is super happy about longitude. He should be. It was much harder to figure out than latitude.

What It Looks Like on A Test:

What is the importance of the line indicated in this graphic? Describe at least three reasons it is important.

1. _____
2. _____
3. _____
4. _____

Latitude and longitude are both measured in degrees, but that's not precise enough. To be more precise, we break them down further into minutes and seconds. So, a longitude coordinate of a place would be listed like this: 73° 56' 21'' W.

This is read "73 degrees, 56 minutes, and 21 seconds West." This the longitude of New York City! Can you look up the longitude of your favorite place?

DEFINE: OASIS

- a fertile or green area in a desert or arid region
- must have a water source, vegetation, and be surrounded by dry area/desert
- most are fed by underground natural springs, called aquifers
- They were critical in trade routes, and they also provide a habitat for animals.

Technically, the entire Nile River is an oasis. It's 22,000 square kilometers, so it may be the largest in the world.

We also use the term "oasis" to describe something that provides a nice contrast, like a park in the middle of a big city. So, lots of restaurants name themselves "oasis."

What It Looks Like on a Test:

If you wanted to be an oasis, you would need to make sure you:

- A. had a water source
- B. were in the middle of an arid area or desert
- C. had vegetation growing around you
- D. all of the above

Own the Oasis!

Imagine that you're starting a new business that is a playground in the middle of a big city with lots of trees and a big fountain. You decide to name it "The Oasis."

Sketch out a logo for your new business.

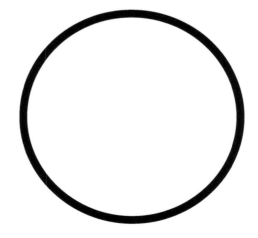

DEFINE: PLACE

- Place is what it's like somewhere.
- It includes the physical features and human characteristics of a location.
- All locations on earth have physical features that set them apart, like climate and landforms and vegetation.
- There are also characteristics that are human made, like highways and houses and stadiums and parks.
- Place can change over time.
- From the Latin *colere,* meaning "to tend, guard; to till, cultivate."

Some places are easy to describe and distinguish, like this famous European city. Others are harder because they're similar to other places.

Watch the trailer of this movie & see if you can describe the place: https://bit.ly/prince-trailer.

What It Looks Like on A Test:

Consider the place of Antarctica. Describe it, including at least two physical features and one feature created by people. Discuss how it has changed over time. How would you have described it 500 years ago?

Make an acrostic poem describing a place you've been.

Name of place _____

P _____

L _____

A _____

C _____

E _____

DEFINE: RELATIVE LOCATION

- where a place is relative to other places, landmarks or points ("It's 30 miles north of New York City", for example)
- The same place will have different relative locations depending upon where it's being described from (if I'm north of it, I'll describe it differently than if I live west of it).
- one of two kinds of location (along with absolute location)

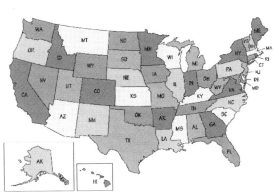

Find Kansas on the map. It is south of Nebraska, east of Colorado, west of Missouri, and north of Oklahoma. It's in the midwestern United States. That's relative location!

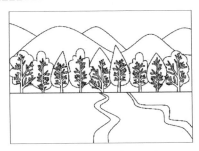

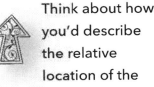 Think about how you'd describe the relative location of the trees.

What It Looks Like on A Test:

Describe the relative location of New Hampshire.

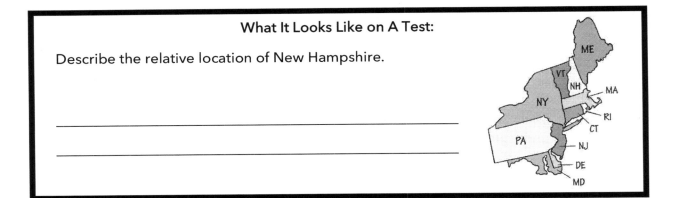

_____

_____

Describe the relative location of your city. What's it close to? Are there other larger cities nearby? Landmarks?

_____

_____

_____

DEFINE: VOLCANO

- a mountain or hill that has a crater or vent that allows lava to erupt or flow from the earth's crust
- formed when magma finds a way to escape from beneath the surface of the earth (magma and lava are the same thing - magma is what it's called when it's below the surface)
- Eruptions can be explosive (where they blast up) or effusive (where they flow).

The most active volcano in the world is Mt. Kilauea in Hawaii. It erupted nearly continuously from 1983 to 2018. It's one of five volcanoes that make up the island of Hawaii.

Volcanoes can be dormant, meaning they haven't erupted in a long time, but they still could. They can also be extinct, meaning they will never erupt again. There are even extinct volcanoes on Mars and Venus!

What It Looks Like on A Test:

Correct this passage. Cross out the words that are not accurate and write in the correct words.

Volcanoes can be active, sleepy, or extinct. When a volcano releases lava, it is called an explosion. When that happens, it can be either explosive or lazy. Volcanoes are found on Earth and no other place. They are formed when lava comes from under the Earth and magma comes out of the volcano.

FIND ALL THESE VOLCANO WORDS!

```
F L O W Q A R Z K R
S R Q U E J L R E W
E E X B V G L A V A
R T E T I L E L I P
U A Y N S A X U T N
P R G A U M T Z C C
T C K M F G I L A M
B E Z R F A N U C H
H H N O E M C A M V
K T Q D F T T R Q A
```

lava

magma

extinct

dormant

active

erupt

effusive

crater

flow

Section III:
Review & Test

10

Review Activities

Learning requires three core pillars: curiosity-fueled introduction to material, quality review activities, and frequent quizzing. It is not an overstatement to estimate that I spend 25% of my prep time planning review and quizzing activities. Although I know this is far more than most teachers, research has proven that it's essential.

The best research on this is available at RetrievalPractice.org. There, the researchers studying what makes for truly effective, deep, lasting learning share their findings and offer lots of practical ideas for teachers. I've mentioned this site before, and I hope you will carve out time to explore their resources. Some of the review activities you will find here are a direct result of their research.

Over the years, I've gathered a number of review activities that I use with Concept Capsules. I'm including my twenty-six favorites here. If I remember where I got it, I list that. Some I made up. Most I've used so long I don't remember where I first heard of it, and my rules may be slightly different because of adjustments I've made over time!

It's important to use a variety of review experiences in order to keep the kids' interest and their brains engaged and active. The Reticular Activating Systems of their brains will tune out if they participate in the same type of game over and over, even if they like the game. It's natural that your students will have some favorites, and it's fine to use those more often, yet even favorites will lose their glow if they are overused.

Ideas for review activities that can be done when five or fewer of the Concept Capsules have been introduced are marked with an asterisk (*).

Some of the activities require quite a bit of competition and may create feelings of anticipation or nervousness in some students. Good. I want that. Dr. Dan Peters, Ph.D., an expert in anxiety in children and the author of *Make Your Worrier a Warrior*, and I wrote an article about how to manage anxiety. One of the most important ideas we shared that apply to teachers was that, "It's empowering for children to fail in safe places . . . systematically desensitizing oneself works somewhat like allergy shots – expose yourself to micro doses of the thing you fear and build tolerance" (Peters, D. & Van Gemert, L., 33). If you're interested, you can read the entire article at https://giftedguru.com/anxiety.

I want my students to get used to those feelings that come before academic challenge because they'll be having challenges when I'm not there, and I want them to learn how to manage that. In their book *Top Dog: The Science of Winning and Losing*, Po Bronson and Ashley Merryman explore the physiology of why we feel anxiety before performance. I highly recommend reading the entire book, but I'll share my greatest takeaway from it with you.

Performance anxiety is not something that we get rid of: it's something we harness the power of. Bronson and Merryman discuss Olympic-level athletes with crushing anxiety before events who know that the biochemistry making the butterflies in your stomach is the same biochemistry that will make you perform at peak.

In a study they reference, students were given a paragraph to read before they took an important test. The paragraph explained that feeling nervous was your body's way of preparing you to perform well, and that if you didn't feel nervous at all, you may not do as well. Guess what? The students who read that did better than those who didn't. So, it's not about eliminating situations that might make them nervous. It's about intentionally creating those experiences so that they develop the skills to manage that nervousness.

All games assume you have clues ready. My suggestion is to create a clue bank in PowerPoint or Google Slides that has clues for all of your Concept Capsules. You can watch a video of how I do that at https://www.giftedguru.com/clue-bank.

The activities are listed in alphabetical order.

---

1. AROUND THE WORLD

PREP/MATERIALS NEEDED:

- Clues. For this activity, I typically prepare my clues in a PowerPoint or in Google Slides presentation. That way, I can just show the clue to the students on my screen as I walk around.

TO PLAY:

1. Begin on one side of the classroom.

2. The first two students stand next to each other.

3. Show the students a clue. The first student to say the answer correctly moves on to challenge the next student.

4. When a student loses a challenge, that student sits in the seat of the opponent who is now moving on to the next student.

5. Each student may only answer once. If neither is able to give a correct answer, save that clue to use at the end of the game and come back to it.

There are a few possible objectives:

- Be the first one to return to your original seat.

- Be the first one to win a certain number of times (you can use markers such as poker chips, pennies, or marbles).

- Time the class to see how quickly the class can make it "Around the World". You can time classes against themselves or each other. We love to have a "time to beat" on the board.

2. BALLOON BLAST

NEEDED:

- Uninflated balloons of different colors (one color per team) with clues to Concept Capsule words inside. Tip: It's easiest to write the clue on a small piece of paper that you roll up and slide in the neck of a balloon.

- Sheet of paper and pen/pencil for each team.

TO PLAY:

1. Have a certain color balloon assigned for each team.

2. Scatter the uninflated balloons (with clues inside) over the floor in one area by you.

3. When you say "GO", one member of each team runs to get a balloon that is their team color and takes it back to their team.

4. Someone on the team blows up the balloon, ties it, and pops the balloon by sitting on it.

5. After they pop the balloon, they get out the clue and write down their best guess.

6. Then, and only then, can another member go get another balloon and begin the process again.

7. When the allotted time is up, you can see who has the most correct answers or you can play until one team finishes first.

Note: This is a vigorous activity. You may wish to play this game in a cafeteria, gym, outside, or other large space!

3. BASEBALL

NEEDED:

- Concept Capsules
- Baseball diamond sketched out on board. If you want to do it digitally, that's fine, too. I find that this activity is just as easily done with a dry erase marker.

TO PLAY:

- Divide class into two teams. Decide what mark will represent which team on the board ("X" and "O" work fine).
- Sketch out a baseball diamond like this:

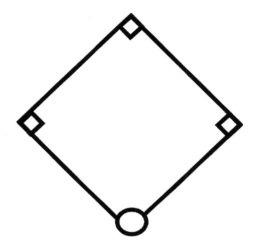

- As in baseball, each team has three outs per inning.
- Students from each team go one at a time.
- Privately show or tell the name of a Concept Capsule to the student whose turn it is.
- That student has up to 20 seconds to define the Concept Capsule. How far around the bases the student gets is determined by how much of that time it takes him/her to define the Capsule.
  - Five seconds or fewer: home run
  - Six to ten seconds: triple
  - Eleven to fifteen seconds: double
  - Sixteen to twenty seconds: single

- Put the mark of that team on the appropriate base. If there are other marks on the baseball diamond (players on other bases), move them the appropriate number of bases forward (simply by erasing and re-writing).

- If the student cannot define the word, the player is out. The team with the most amount of runs at the end of the game is the winning team.

4. BINGO

NEEDED:

- Clues

- List of Concept Capsules in play

- Bingo board for each student (in *Templates* section). While I've included a Bingo board template, I'd highly recommend the website https://BingoBaker.com. BingoBaker lets you create Bingo boards, which is great. However, its real power is that it prints out a variety of boards, so that your students don't have the same board. I have the paid version (which is a one-time, very low price), but the free version will work just fine.

- Pen/Pencil for each student

- Markers for each student (I typically use bulk generic Cheerios® that I place in paper bathroom cups).

- Decide ahead of time what kind of Bingo you're going to use. In addition to the traditional horizontal, vertical, or diagonal 5-in-a-row lines, you can also choose to do any of these variations:

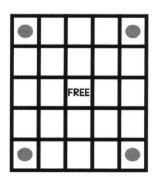

This version is called "4 Corners" (for obvious reasons). You could create a variation of it by picking any four (or more) specific spots on the board that are the winning spots.

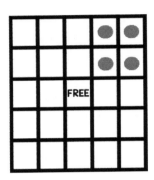

This version is called "Postage Stamp."

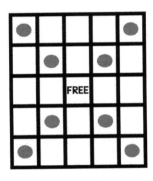

This version is called "X Marks the Spot."

- Decide on a prize, if any. You don't need to have a prize every time, or you can simply have everyone clap or give some other recognition for a student getting Bingo.

TO PLAY:

1. List all of the words in play in a way that all students can see them. I will usually put them up on a screen. These are the Concept Capsule words you're reviewing.

2. Students fill in their Bingo boards with the words any way they want.

3. You call out the clue to each word.

4. They have to wait until you count to ten, and then they can put a marker on their card. I do this because I want them to think, not just react.

5. Bingo wins.

6. When a student calls *"Bingo!,"* ask them to list the words they have. Do not respond to individual words – just say, "Yes, that's Bingo" or "No, that's not Bingo" when they're done listing the Concept Capsules they're marked. That way, if they are incorrect play can continue, rather than having lots of other kids mark words they didn't really have.

Adaptation for when you have fewer than 24 Capsules introduced: Because 24 Capsules are required to fill a board with unique words in each space (assuming the center square is FREE), you have to adapt this game until you've introduced that many Capsules.

To do this, decide how many duplicate uses of each word you'll allow. For example, if you've introduced eight Concept Capsules, you could allow students to use each one three times and no more, or if you've introduced seven, you could allow three words to be used four times and four words to be used three times.

You can allow the use of "up to" so many times to accommodate trickier numbers. The key is that you must have different clues for each of those uses, meaning that if you have words that may appear on the board four times, you need to have four different clues for that Capsule. (One advantage of Bingo Baker is that it lets you make smaller boards!)

5. BUCKET BRIGADE*

NEEDED:

- Copies of Concept Capsule quizzes and/or tests (one for each student) cut apart

- Buckets labeled with numbers to match the number of questions. These don't need to be real buckets. I use small containers I get at Dollar Tree. (If there are ten questions, there would be ten buckets labeled 1 – 10) placed on desks or tables in the room.

- I've made some labels for you to use. I made 25 labels, which will be more than enough for this game! They are in pretty, glittery goodness, and there is a set of them for you to use in this or any other way you wish. To make more (there are two blanks), you can match the font. It is KG Blank Space Solid.

You can download them at

https://www.giftedguru.com/bucket-labels.

TO PLAY:

- Place the copies of the questions on desks where there are no buckets.

- Students move around (in any order), pick up a question, answer it, then bring the paper to you to check their answers.

- If the question is answered correctly, initial their question slip.

- They then write their name on the question slip, fold it up, and put it in the bucket that matches that question number.

- If the student gets it wrong, he/she can have one more chance to find the right answer, coming back to you again to check. If the question is still answered incorrectly, you put a check mark on it, and the student saves it for further review.

- When everyone is done (or randomly throughout – it's up to you) draw slips out of the buckets for small prizes.

If you have too many students lined up to be checked at one time, you can have a few students be assigned as "checkers."

VARIATION: Have a single bucket in which to turn in slips. Rather than having the teacher check all of the answers, select student "checkers." If correct, the checker writes his/her name on the paper, as does the student answering, and then turns the slip in to the bucket. Every few minutes, draw a slip from the bucket for a small prize.

Note: This game was modified from an idea at http://thirdgradeexperience.blogspot.com.

6. CHALKBOARD RELAY*

NEEDED:

- Clues

- Chalkboard/whiteboard

- Chalk/dry erase markers

- Two chairs

TO PLAY:

- Divide the class into teams. Set up 2 chairs at one end of the room and a chalk board at the other with a line drawn vertically down the middle and 2 pieces of chalk in the tray.

- This is a relay race. One person from each team sits in a chair.

- Say the clue.

- As soon as the person sitting in the chair thinks of the answer, they run to the other end of the room and write the answer on the board. If they run to the board and do not immediately start writing, they cannot get a point. They are not supposed to get out of the chair until they know what they are going to write.

- The team that writes the answer first and correctly gets one point. The kids rejoin their team, and the next person on the team sits on the chair.

- You need to stand next to the board so you can see who writes the answer first and correctly.

7. CONCENTRATION*

NEEDED:

- Clues

- Matching Concept Capsules

- Print both of these on either on 8 ½ x 11 brightly colored cardstock for a full-room activity or in a smaller size for table- or desktop play, laminated for durability, if desired. Personally, I like to have both sets.

Note: I use the colored cardstock for durability and because the color blocks the clues from bleeding through. If you prefer, you can print them on white paper and glue them on to construction paper or cardstock.

TO PLAY:

- Lay clues and Capsules in random order in a grid on the floor face down.

- Let students try to make matches. If the match is unsuccessful, the student lays both cards back down, face down, and play continues with the next team or player.

- You may play this as teams or individuals.

8. FLY SWATTER GAME*

NEEDED:

- Concept Capsules written one per page on 8 ½ x 11 sheets of paper

- One fly swatter per team (I get mine at Dollar Tree)

TO PLAY:

- Hang clues up on an accessible wall in the room (meaning a wall that students can get to without running into desks, so you may have to shove desks around for this one).

- Divide your class into teams of at least 3 people per team.

- The more teams there are, the more action there is (for good or ill!).

- The teacher calls out a clue, and the first one to run up and hit the correct word with the fly swatter wins a point for their team.

- You can have more than one clue per Capsule, so the same word may be used over and over.

9. GRUDGEBALL

NEEDED:

- Clues
- Nerf®-type basketball game
- Masking/painter's tape
- White/chalkboard
- Chalk/markers

TO PLAY:

- Set up the basketball game in the room.
- Use the tape to set up one- and two-point lines on the floor.
- Divide the class into five or six teams, depending upon the size of your class and how quickly you want the game to go (fewer teams = quicker game).
- Divide the board into columns, one column for each team.
- In each column, draw ten "X's." Give each team a clue. If the team guesses correctly, two things happen:
  1. They get the Basketball Bonus. A player from the team shoots the basketball from either the one- or two-point line. If they make the shot, they get those points as extra erasures in step 2 below.
  2. They get to erase two X's from the board for their correct guess, taking them away from another team (they may not take their own X's off), plus they erase X's for any additional points they gained in the Basketball bonus, for a total possible of four erasures. They may take the X's from the same team, or they may divide up the erasures from different teams.
- The object of the game is to be the last team with X's on the board or to be the team with the most X's remaining when time expires.
- If a team loses all of its X's, it can get back on the board by getting a question correct and then take a basketball shot. They can then get up to four X's back.
- Decide ahead of time, based upon the emotional maturity of the class, if you are going to allow teams to create alliances to try to eliminate a particular team. You may also wish to discuss ahead of time that this is a game and not personal. The object is to play, and if kids let their feelings get hurt, they will have less fun.

Variations:

Variation 1) If the team whose turn it is does not answer correctly, you may wish to allow other teams to try to steal the points. They can do this by answering correctly and then taking a shot at the basket. They must get the question correct AND successfully take a shot. They then can take away three or four X's (depending upon the distance from which they took the shot) from the team(s) of their choice. If they do not make the shot, they cannot take away X's.

Variation 2) You can have students answer individually and then, if they cannot answer alone, you can allow them to ask for help from their team for the possibility to erase a single X, rather than two.

The idea for this game came from http://toengagethemall.blogspot.com.

10. HOT SEAT

NEEDED:

- Clues
- Chair
- White/chalkboard

TO PLAY:

- Have a student sit in the front of the classroom on a chair facing away from the board.
- On the board, write a Concept Capsule word (or display on a screen) so it cannot be seen by the person in the chair.
- The person in the chair (the "hotseat") asks "yes" or "no" questions of the class to try to figure out which Concept Capsule is written on the board.
- The person can ask up to ten questions. The questions may not be "Is it this word _____?" They must be more general (see rules for Twenty Questions for more ideas on this).
- You can give a small prize or extra credit point to the student if he/she is able to figure it out within the ten question limit.

11. JENGA®

NEEDED:

- Clues

- Jenga® games (at least one, but you can use as many as you want, need not be the "real" one)

TO PLAY:

- Divide students into as many teams as you have Jenga games.

- If you have one game, simply play as a whole class.

- Build the Jenga tower(s).

- Each student takes a turn responding to the clue. If the student answers correctly, the student can remove a piece from the Jenga tower anywhere below the highest completed story. They can begin or add to a new story on the top of the tower. Remember, you must complete a story before starting a new one.

- Players may only use one hand to remove or stack the block, and they can only do one block per turn. They can test the looseness or tightness of the block, but if you jar a block out of position, you have to put it back where it was (still just one hand!).

- After the block is positioned in its new spot on top of the tower, wait ten seconds to see if the tower falls.

- The last player to successfully add a piece to the tower before it collapses/falls over wins (so the person's whose turn it was before the person's turn who knocked it down).

12. MR. POTATO HEAD®

NEEDED:

- You will need at least two Mr. Potato Heads

- Dry erase board

- Dry erase marker for each team

- Clues

TO PLAY:

- Divide the class into two teams (or as many teams as you have Mr. Potato Heads).

- Give clues. If the team can produce the correct Capsule to match the clue (writing it on the dry erase board) in ten seconds, they get to add a piece to their Mr. Potato Head.

- The first team to completely build Mr. Potato Head wins.

13. POST IT

NEEDED:

- Sticky notes with Concept Capsules written on them (one per student, may duplicate Concept Capsules)

TO PLAY:

- Place a sticky note on the back of each student without letting him/her see the note.

- Students then pair up, with each student asking the other a yes/no question to try to identify which Concept Capsule is written on their note.

- They ask each student only one question, and then find another student to ask. They may not ask, "Am I such-and-such?" They must ask only clue questions.

- You can play for a winner, or you can play where as soon as a player figures out their own Concept Capsule, they assist a classmate.

14. QR CODES

NEEDED:

- QR codes with clues (see description below)
- Paper on which to record responses

TO PLAY:

- Scatter the QR codes around the room on the walls and/or desks.

- Have students scan the codes and then write the corresponding Concept Capsule on their sheet (the codes reveal clues).

- To make it more difficult, use some that have not yet been introduced and instruct students to make note of those as well.

Note: QR codes often link to websites, but you may not know that they can be scanned to read plain text. You can use a site like https://www.qrcode-tiger.com to generate the codes. It's so quick – you'll be astonished!

To see what I mean about scanning to read text, use a QR scanner to scan this code:

15. SNOWBALL

NEEDED:

- A blank sheet of paper for each student

TO PLAY:

- Each student writes a clue or definition of a Concept Capsule (using the Capsules they have) on the piece of paper, along with their name, and then balls it up like a snowball.
- Once everyone has done this, let them throw the "snowballs" at each other (Gently, Gently!).
- Each person then picks up a snowball, smooths it out, and tries to guess which Concept Capsule the clue corresponds to.
- The person writes the Concept Capsule they think it is on the paper and then checks with the person who created the snowball to see if they are correct.
- If they are correct, they crumple it back up and students make a pile of the correct snowballs. (You can be the referee if there is disagreement among the students.)

16. STARMAN*

NEEDED:

- Display surface (board or document camera)
- Marker

TO PLAY:

- This is a school-friendly version of Hangman. Draw a "T" chart on the board/display on the document camera.

- Select a Concept Capsule and draw the number of dashes that there are letters in the word on the board or document camera.

- Let students suggest letters that they think occur in the word. If the student correctly guesses a letter that appears in the word, fill in that letter above the dash.

- If the word does not contain that letter, draw one section of the Starman (see diagram).

- A student may use his/her turn to guess the word. If the guess is incorrect, add another segment of Starman.

- If the word is correctly guessed or completed before the six segments of the Starman are drawn, the students score a point.

- If not, Starman scores a point.

- Use tally marks to note the points on the T chart you drew.

Note: Starman is a five pointed star with a circle for a head above it. It's easiest to begin with the star, and then draw the circle, and it's easiest to begin with the left-hand downward line of the star to create scale, but you can draw the star in any order.

17. SURVIVOR

NEEDED:

- Clues

- ½ sheet of paper and pen for each student to draw a Starman (*see* "Starman" above).

- 5-10 index cards for challenges

- Dry erase boards

- Dry erase markers

- Draw a complete Starman on the board, adding circles for hands and feet. This will give you ten steps until elimination.

TO PLAY:

- Read a clue and then begin to count down from ten, having students stand up before you reach zero with the correct response written on their dry erase board.

- Any student who doesn't stand in time or who has an incorrect response draws a part of Starman on the ½ sheet of paper.

- Play resumes with another clue.

- After five clues, have a challenge (give a difficult clue). Any guessing the wrong word on a challenge is off of the island.

- Continue for five more clues, then challenge again.

- Repeat until you are down to two survivors. Hold a tribal council where the two remaining players play rock-paper-scissors to determine the survivor. The survivor gets a 100 Grand candy bar.

18. TABOO®

NEEDED:

- Cards with clues (The cards will have a Concept Capsule at the top, and then five "taboo" words listed underneath. See example.)

- Timer

- A buzzer or whistle or bell

PSYCHOLOGIST
therapy
mind
counseling
couch
Freud

TO PLAY:

- Divide the class into two teams.

- The first team is given the stack of clue cards face down.

- One person is the describer.

- On a signal, the describer turns the card over and describe the vocabulary word without using any of the "taboo" words or any part of the word itself.

- If he/she says either of those, the teacher buzzes the buzzer, and the other team gets that card for a point.

- Play until the timer goes off (1 minute), then give the team two points for every word they got in time.

- They may skip words they don't know and put them at the bottom of the pile face down. After you have tallied the team's score, the next team has its turn.

Note: In the *Templates* section, Taboo clues are provided for all the Content Capsules in the book.

19. TWENTY QUESTIONS*

NEEDED:

- 20 Questions Check Off (in *Templates* section)

TO PLAY:

- Students will have 20 questions in which to guess the Concept Capsule.

- The teacher does not have to be the answerer – a student may do this as well.

- Responses can be any one of the following words: yes, no, usually, sometimes, or rarely.

Note: This review game is particularly easy because you don't need to create clues!

20. TRASHKETBALL

NEEDED:

- Clues
- Small dry erase boards
- Dry erase markers
- Trashcan
- Masking or painter's tape
- Small soft ball

TO PLAY:

- Divide students into teams of three or four.

- Give one small dry erase board and marker to each team.

- Set up the trashcan a couple of feet in front of a wall.

- Using the masking or painter's tape, set up three lines: one point, two points, and three points, with each line farther away from the basket.

- Give a clue for a Concept Capsule. Every team writes their answer on the dry erase board (one answer per team).

- Call time (after however long you want to give – decide in advance how long this will be) and have all of the teams show their answers simultaneously.

- Every team with a correct response earns a point and gets to take a shot into the trashcan with the ball for possible extra points.

- Everyone on the team rotates taking shots (they can't have a designated shooter – they must take turns).

- Record each team's points on the board.

- When you are nearly done with the time you are going to spend, give them one more question and let them wager their points. They can wager some, all, or none of their points.

- They write their wager on their dry erase board, and come up and hand that board to you, keeping it secret from the rest of the class, until every team has shot.

- As each team's representative takes this final shot, record on the dry erase if the shot was successful or not by circling the points if the shot was successful. Once every team has taken this final shot, record the results of the wagers. This part is so suspenseful!

21. TWISTYWORDS*

NEEDED:

- Clues

- Twister® game

- Concept Capsule words printed out & laminated

- Velcro on Twister circles on the play mat and backs of Concept Capsules

TO PLAY:

- Attach the Concept Capsules to the circles on the Twister vinyl play mat.

- Have two students play the game, only rather than using the spinner, give clues to the Concept Capsules that they have to identify and place their hands/feet on the appropriate circle.

- To play this when you have fewer Capsules introduced, you can make multiple circles the same Concept Capsule (this works well all of the time, actually, because it makes it possible to reach them all!).

22. VOCABULARY TOSS

NEEDED:

- Clues

- Chalk/whiteboard
- Small soft ball
- Trashcan or bucket

TO PLAY:

- Divide class into two teams and have them line up single file in two parallel lines.
- Ask the first player on one of the teams to respond to a clue. If he/she is correct, the team gets a point and the player gets to shoot at the trashcan or bucket.
- If he/she makes it into the container, the team gets an additional point.
- Record the points on the board. He/she then goes to the end of the line of his/her team.
- If the player answers incorrectly or does not know the answer, the player in first position (and only that player) on the other team can answer for the chance to toss the ball (no point is earned for answering correctly) for a chance at a point. That does not count as the turn for that player (meaning that he/she does not rotate and gets a chance to answer the next question).
- Play until everyone has had a turn or time runs out.

23. WINTER WARMER

NEEDED:

- Clues
- Winter clothing items (hat, scarves, gloves, warm socks, boots, parka, ski goggles, etc.)

TO PLAY:

- Prepare for each team a hat, scarf, a pair of gloves, a pair of woolly socks and a pair of boots. If you have ski goggles or other winter wear, you can use that, too.
- Choose a representative for each team and have them sit on chairs in front of the class.
- Read the clue to the team. If the team answers correctly, the representative at the front dons on item (gloves, socks and boots may go on in pairs in the interest of time or if you have fewer clues).
- The first team to wear everything wins.

24. WORD JUMBLES

NEEDED:

- Jumbled Concept Capsules – To create these, use a free site such as https://www.education.com/worksheet-generator/reading/word-scramble/ to scramble the words.

- Pen/pencil for each student

TO PLAY:

- Students try to unscramble the Concept Capsule jumbled words.

- You can have them work with partners or in teams.

- Note: This one does not require the creation of clues, but it is a more shallow activity. I do this just as the most basic of review activities, and I do not use it with students with language processing issues.

25. ZAP!

NEEDED:

- Clues

- Zap! scoring cards (download at https://www.giftedguru.com/zap-game-printable)

- Paper or white board to record running score

TO PLAY:

- Divide class into two or more teams.

- Shuffle the scoring cards and stack them face down (or use Zap! board as shown below).

- Decide which team goes first, and then give that team the first question. Use your normal methods to choose whom to call on (random, popsicle sticks, in order, etc.).

- If the student answers correctly, the student draws a scoring card and then adjusts the team score according to the scoring card.

- If the team has no points and the card says, "double the score," the score remains at zero.

- Scores can go into negative numbers.

- If the student answers incorrectly, the question goes to the next team, who decides on the answer as a team. If that team answers correctly within a time limit you set, that team takes the top scoring card in their deck.

- Because many of the cards actually lose points, "winning" is not that straightforward. You may wish to give students the option to not choose a card if they answer correctly as the card may be costly!

Note: This is a student favorite! It's a must-try! You can play with a stack of cards, although I use it so often that I've made this board with black foam core board from the dollar store and library card pockets from Amazon. I print the cards out, cut them up, and slide them in the pockets.

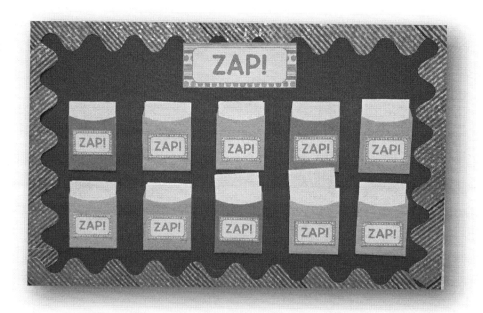

This screenshot shows the template cards and a sample of the download available at https://www.giftedguru.com/zap-game-printable.

26. ZINGED!

NEEDED:

- Popsicle sticks or tongue depressors with Concept Capsules written on them (one Concept Capsule per stick) and one with "Zinged!" written on it

TO PLAY:

- A student draws a stick and asks the class a question about the Concept Capsule without giving it away.
- If the class figures out the corresponding question, the student giving the clue has earned a point for the class.
- If the class cannot figure it out, a point is lost.
- If a student draws the *Zinged!* stick, all of the sticks go back in the container and all points are lost.
- The goal is for the class to have a positive point total when the time is over.

Note: This is another low-prep game, because all you need is the Concept Capsule written on the stick and one stick with *Zinged!*. You don't need clues.

ADDITIONAL IDEAS:

Virtually any game can be adapted for use with Concept Capsules. Think of the games you like to play and ponder about how you could incorporate them into your vocabulary review time. Games such as *Jeopardy!*, *Wheel of Fortune*, and Battleship make wonderful games. Some of them take time to set up, but once done can be used for years.

11

How to Quiz & Test the Concept Capsules

The quizzes and tests are important. Let me explain why, for those of you who resist frequent quizzing. I came across a study done by Edwina Abbott in 1909 (not a typo) called *On the Analysis of the Factor of Recall in the Learning Process*. Sounds like a nail-biter, doesn't it? I was intrigued, though, because it showed the idea of review has been known to be effective in learning for a very, very long time. Her findings supported those of Hermann Ebbinghaus (the Forgetting Curve guy).

Later, I read about how Washington University in St. Louis did a study to figure out the most effective method of studying a foreign language with flashcards. (Let's face it: for many students, academic vocabulary may as well be a foreign language.)

The study was trying to determine if it were better to stop studying the words you already knew, removing those cards from the stack, or to keep even the already-mastered words in the deck from which students were studying.

What did they find? It didn't matter whether you took the cards out or left them in the stack. What did? Frequent quizzing of all of the words, meaning that no word was safe to stop studying because they could appear at any time on any quiz.

That study, and many, many other follow-up studies have found the same thing: *the brain values what it thinks it will be tested on.*

This study had a profound impact on my teaching, as I began to include questions from previous assessments in every quiz or test. No information was forgettable. Students knew that the test on one novel would have questions requiring them to analyze previously read works. They didn't ask me what would be on the test. They knew the answer: everything.

Student achievement rose, and not just by the arbitrary measure of grades, but also by the quality of the class discussion and the students' effortless use of the ideas.

If you're interested in more about the science of this and how it looks in classrooms, I strongly recommend the book written by researcher Pooja Agarwal and Patrice Bain, *Powerful teaching: unleash the science of learning*. There is also an incredible amount of fantastic, free material for teachers at the https://RetrievalPractice.org website.

It's not just vocabulary. All learning benefits from this and associated strategies.

Quizzing

As discussed in Chapter 2, quizzes are essential. They come in three forms:

1. Short, weekly Concept Capsule quizzes (approximately 5 questions)

2. Longer, less frequent Concept Capsule quizzes (between 10 – 25 questions)

3. Inclusion of Concept Capsule questions on other, unrelated quizzes (a single question, usually given as a bonus point)

It's vital that these quizzes are low stakes. Students must feel that the quizzes are a chance to practice, not fail.

When a quiz only has five questions, it's not far from perfect to failing. To avoid that dynamic, I do not count the grade for every quiz by itself. I'd end up with too many grades in my gradebook, as well as making the quizzes too high-risk. It's a central tenet of retrieval practice that the quizzes must be low-stakes.

In the gradebook, the quizzes are recorded based on how many the student got correct, rather than a percentage. In the name of the quiz, I'll put in how many questions were on that quiz, so it would listed in the gradebook as "CC Quiz #4/5" or "CC Quiz #7/6." The number after the slanted line indicated how many questions there were. At the end of the grading period, I add all of those numbers up, giving me a total possible. I then figure out how many total points the student earned. So, if there were 36 possible, and the student got 30 correct, the student would earn an 83% on a single grade called "Concept Capsule Quizzes" that is entered in the grade book, and the individual grades are marked as not counting. Our digital gradebooks can calculate this for me, but if yours can't, a spreadsheet will work beautifully and quickly.

Students are one of best sources for quiz questions, and just like I have a PowerPoint with my Concept Capsule clues to use in review activities, I also have a bank of quiz questions I keep on hand. I do not hesitate to repeat the same question occasionally, especially with a little change.

Quiz questions take all forms except True/False. I'm not a fan of True/False questions in general, and I rarely use them. Question types will include:

- Multiple choice

- Short answer

- Fill-in-the-blank

- Ordering

- Matching

- Likert scale

Having a variety of question types keeps the quizzes feeling fresh. You can either mix the styles on a single quiz, or rotate types of quizzes, week by week.

The only one of these question types that may not be familiar is the Likert scale question. You've probably seen Likert scales before. They're the questions that ask you if you strongly agree, agree, are neutral, disagree, or strongly disagree. For a Concept Capsule, that would look like this:

Your parents tell you that you are going on vacation to a plateau. From this, you know that you are probably going someplace surrounded by water.

Strongly agree   Agree   No opinion   Disagree   Strongly disagree

I'm a big fan of this style of question. In this case, I would accept either "Disagree" or "Strongly disagree" as acceptable answers. This means that students have a greater chance of giving a correct response. For some reason, students love these questions. Perhaps because they feel like simply an opinion, they seem to be less threatening or intimidating than other question types, though they are in reality no easier.

When preparing to write this book, I dug through my old files, looking for examples of some of the first quizzes I'd ever given over Concept Capsules. I found this AP Government quiz that is so old it wasn't even stored digitally! I had to scan it in! I considered retyping it, but I think there's value in seeing this is from a real, live teacher with real, live students. This is real.

Let's look at this quiz closely, so that you can see some of the strategies I use to make the quizzes a source of pleasure and good feelings, not a *Gotcha!*

I began the quiz with three straightforward multiple choice questions. Notice that on

Concept Quiz 1

1. Which of the following describes a psychological rather than institutional concept? This is the way a people view themselves.
   a. regime
   b. nation
   c. state
   d. government

2. This is a political system in which citizens enjoy basic civil and political rights, most important political leaders are elected in free and fair elections, and leaders are accountable under a rule of law.
   a. socialist state
   b. democracy
   c. totalitarian regime
   d. parliamentary

3. The exclusive right to have control over an area or people is called
   a. power
   b. authoritarian rule
   c. sovereignty
   d. authority

the first question, I gave the students an extra hint (*This is the way a people view themselves.*) Especially when learning is young and fragile, I will often hint. My job is not to intimidate; it's to encourage. I want them to feel that I'm in their corner, helping them to do the best they can. I know you're curious: the answer to that question is *B, nation.*

After those first questions, I move on to what is my students' favorite type of question after Likert scale questions (and sometimes I combine the types). These are the scenario-based multiple choice questions, where I make the question some short, silly story. I want to hear students laugh when they are taking these quizzes. No laughter? I didn't do my job. When one student laughs, the others are incentivized to keep going, hoping to get to a funny question.

4. Susan lives in a country where she is allowed to join the Paris Hilton Fan Club and the Future Independents group without the government interfering, even though she's stupid and her friends wish she couldn't even vote. Her type of country is called what?
   a. civilian run
   b. civil society
   c. civilization
   d. civil union

5. Steve's country is one big thing without any separation into smaller units like states. He never has to say the Texas pledge, and he feels like he's missing out. He lives under which type of system?
   a. Mickey Mouse
   b. federal
   c. unitary
   d. united

6. Joe Bob Billy wants to open a store that sells redneck wear and souvenirs. He bought a trailer to set up his shop, but he can't because in his country, the state owns everything. What kind of economy is that?
   a. anti-entrepreneurial
   b. smart
   c. command
   d. market

I love hearing students talk about the quizzes in the hall. I don't even care if they're talking about it with other students who haven't yet taken the quiz. It's all about a good experience to me.

One note about question 5. Do you see the answer choice *Mickey Mouse*? That seems like a throw-away answer, doesn't it? But it's not. Earlier, my students had learned about Nebraska's unicameral state legislature. I had let the students vote on what we should call that, and they voted "Mickey Mouse." This answer choice gave them a reminder of that piece of knowledge, connecting it to a previously formed neural pathway. I just love teaching.

The rest of the quiz is similar until the last question that is short answer. Notice that it has no number. That's because this is the first time I've quizzed this concept in short answer form. I'm checking to see if they can do it, and I'll share out great responses with the class later, but I will not count it wrong yet. Remember: low stakes!

7. Patty thinks her senator is having an affair with his secretary. She cares because she is the senator's wife. She thinks about hiring a private detective, but doesn't want to waste her money in case he IS cheating and she has to dump him. Instead, she requests all of his email in a freedom of information request. He has to turn it all over to her because their country operates under this principle:
    a. monogamy
    b. transparency
    c. honesty
    d. civilian control

8. William III became the king upon the death of his father, William II. His son, William IV, will be the king after him. They have this kind of legitimacy:
    a. charismatic
    b. rational-legal
    c. royal
    d. traditional

9. Even though Sharon isn't an elected official, she does work for a non-governmental agency that has a lot of influence on the Department of Health and Home Shopping Networks. She is part of what we would call the what?
    a. government
    b. state
    c. regime
    d. nation

10. Matthew lives in Sweater, a cold country that used to be a part of the Soviet Union. Although they have free, fair, and competitive elections, Sweater is missing some of the other qualities you need to have a liberal democracy. This is called what?
    a. substantive democracy
    b. too bad
    c. illiberal democracy
    d. democracy light

11. Mark is trying to Josh the value of a civil society. Josh isn't buying it, even when Mark explains all but which of these advantages?
    a. People can organize and work to achieve a common goal.
    b. People can learn that process is as important as immediate results.
    c. Ability to work with others to achieve a common goal.
    d. Important route into politics for the wealthy and powerful

Define civil society. Compare the level of civil society in China to that of Great Britain.

Some of you may be surprised by question 7 (Patty and her cheating senator). This is an AP class with only 11th & 12th graders in it. I wouldn't include a question like that in a quiz for younger grades. It was one of their favorites, though. The rest of the semester, students were lamenting, "Poor Patty."

Notice that I sometimes do throw in a ridiculous answer choice (like the "too bad" in question 10). I don't do it every question or it loses its power to get the kids to chuckle or grunt in amusement.

As you can see, the quizzes are not only aligned with the research on effective teaching and learning. They are a source of fun, team building, and class culture building. The students would legitimately be sad to not have them.

Even if you choose not to use the Concept Capsule method, I hope you can take away some ideas about quizzing.

Testing

In addition to adding a Concept Capsule in as a bonus question on every assessment I give students, there is also one major test per semester that is solely on the Capsules.

As with the quizzes, these are typically greatly anticipated by students. Going in, they know this:

- They have all the knowledge they need to do well.

- The test will not be designed to trick them.

- They will laugh and have a good time taking it.

How do they know this? They have been told that by me, of course, but they have experienced it over and over in the quizzes.

To create some excitement around the test and to make it feel more like a celebration than a stressful experience, I do some or all of the following:

- Decorate the room with balloons from the dollar store

- Twist streamers from the dollar store from the door jam into the hallway, taping them to the floor (student favorite)

- Play special music as students come into class

- Sprinkle funny quotes, comics, and inside jokes throughout the test

- Dress up (I usually choose Professor Mcgonagall – I even have her wand! I have a friend who dresses as Darth Vader.)

- Blow bubbles as students walk in the room

- Give out good luck charms (I give pennies.)

You don't need to do any of this. It's what I do to make it feel like a different experience than they are used to with big tests. Find whatever works for you and your students.

It seems like fun and games, doesn't it? Yet this is a very difficult test. Here are sample questions from several grade levels (I've taught both elementary and high school, so I have a wide range of samples from which to choose.)

Third Grade Examples:

1. If you were a farmer, describe why it would be better to live near a delta than a glacier.

2. What would happen to a food web if the apex predator became extinct? Describe at least three possible outcomes.

3. The word "dividend" is no longer available. Come up with a new word for this, and explain why your word is a good choice.

Fifth Grade Examples:

1. Your rocket ship has launched! Your lead scientist tells you it reached all the way to the lithosphere! How exciting! Or is it? Explain.

2. Javier writes a memoir. Describe three things you'd expect to find in it.

3. You want to fit as much ice cream as possible into your container. The ice cream store clerk offers you a typical cone or a cylinder. Which one would give you more ice cream if they had the same base and the same height?

9th Grade Examples:

1. Describe why the terms "immigration" and "emigration" make more sense when you understand the etymology.

2. Your dad's getting all fancy with allowance after listening to too much Dave Ramsey on the radio. He asks you if you would you rather be paid an allowance with a base of 4 and an exponent of 3 or a base of 2 and an exponent of 6? What do you answer?

3. D'Quan loves his graphing calculator so much that he gives it a name and thinks it really likes him. Is this anthropomorphism or personification?

12th Grade Examples:

1. Breanna's favorite class is calculus (of course). You overhear her talking at lunch, trying to explain something to the principal, who, sadly, never took calculus. You hear this, "Well, Ms. Jimenez, a function is _____ if it is defined at $x = a$, meaning $f(a)$ is a real number…" You don't hear the rest, but you instantly know that that the word that goes in the blank is _____.

2. Stephan has been paying super careful attention in economics. He asked someone out to prom, and then the week later, he found out that the person he really wanted to ask broke up with her date and was available. His friend tried to tell him he should ditch his date and ask the person he really wanted, but Stephan understands that when you make one choice, you often give up another. "Dude, he said, there's an _____ _____ in asking out one person."

3. Mauricio loves Beowulf. I mean loves it. He's reading along and comes across the break in the middle of a line indicated by this symbol: //. He instantly thinks of a Shakespeare play that explored honor and was based on Roman history. Why did that play occur to him?

How many did you know? Hopefully you can see that even the questions asked in the scenario style have significant substance to them. They're not easy. You have to know your stuff, and you have to be able to use it in different applications. It's not a coincidence that many of the scenarios involve students' "real lives." It's important that they know they will use these words in more than just the classroom.

Wrapping Up

The quizzes and tests are not only a key part of the learning process, but they are also an opportunity to create your classroom culture. Done well, they will help your students learn the Concept Capsules, of course, but they may have the added benefit of changing their minds about tests and quizzes in general. When we have multiple, successful experiences with assessment, we can change our minds about our assessment prowess.

While it was the research that led me to frequent quizzing, it was the effect on students' attitudes that made me fall in love with it. It spilled over into every quiz and assessment in the class. Hopefully, the same will be true of your students.

12

Conclusion

If you read the Concept Capsule Origin Story at the beginning of this book, you read this line:

Concept Capsules are one-page introductions to the academic vocabulary of a discipline, all laid out in the same pattern, shared with students slowly over time and frequently reviewed – what I call in class "playing with."

Now that you have finished the book and read everything I could think of to tell you about them, I hope that the beautiful simplicity of that single-sentence description resonates with you. It truly is that simple. Things do not have to be complicated to work well.

It shouldn't surprise us that this method is effective because it completely aligns with the research on optimal vocabulary instruction. There's a confidence that comes to educators who align their teaching to quality research that has stood the test of time. It is my hope that that confidence will fill your classroom, spilling over from you to your students.

I have always taught in integrated, diverse schools. Typically, a third of my students are learning English as their second language. Another third speak a range of dialects common in the South. For me, a strong vocabulary is an equity issue for my students. Linguistic bias is a way that implicit racism and stereotypes manifest themselves (Beukeboom, 2014). As an educator, I want to do all I can to arm my students against this bias.

Teaching in Texas made this even more urgent. The work of Dennis Preston on dialect persuaded me of how important this is. In a study he did in 1999 of 150 Michigan residents, he asked participants to rank the "correctness" of the English spoken in all 50 states. The area that ranked lowest? The South. Alabama was dead last, in case you're wondering. My students, both white and students of color, are fighting this bias. That "y'all" makes you seem nice, but also benignly stupid.

Even after the Great Migration led many African-Americans northward towards better, industrialized jobs after the Civil War, the South still remained – and remains to this day – the area of our country with the largest concentration of African-Americans (about 60% of African-Americans live in the South). That means that they fight both racial *and* linguistic prejudice.

Even the best vocabulary method will not change how other people feel about my students by itself, but the confidence the students gain from knowing that the power of language – of academic language – is theirs for the taking is powerful. When they go to college, they will take the confidence with them.

Whatever is against your students, whether it be race, ethnicity, social status, poverty, a lack of parental support, or any of the other issues that plague our youth, words are what empower us. Everywhere I have lived, language has been a status marker. This isn't an American issue. It was the same in Germany when I lived there. As a species, we're language snobs.

Concept Capsules won't change an accent or others' perceptions of it, but they do have the power to make students feel the confidence that comes from knowing that whatever discipline they decide to pursue, the language of that discipline is open to them. They will recognize – perhaps before their peers – the importance of that academic vocabulary. They will know how to learn it, how to practice it, and how to own it.

Many of my students report back to me that they created their own Concept Capsules when they got to college. It's a portable method.

As with anything else, the longer you do it, the more natural it will feel. As you see your students grow in skill and confidence, you will gain a deep sense of satisfaction and accomplishment. There is a very good change that is why you became a teacher. I know it's why I did. Well, I really like office supplies, but mostly it was because I wanted to be an enabler of the best kind.

It is my deepest hope that this method will work for you and your students as it has for me and mine. If it does, I hope you'll tell me about it.

Section 4:
Appendix

Templates

20 QUESTIONS!

PUT AN "X" IN EACH BOX AS THE QUESTIONS ARE ASKED!

1	2	3	4	5
6	7	8	9	10
11	12	13	14	15
16	17	18	19	20

20 QUESTIONS!

PUT AN "X" IN EACH BOX AS THE QUESTIONS ARE ASKED!

1	2	3	4	5
6	7	8	9	10
11	12	13	14	15
16	17	18	19	20

TABOO® Clues

Here are Taboo clues for all of the Concept Capsules in the book. I typically create these clues when I add create the Concept Capsule. That just turns out to be quicker than going back once they're all done and creating a big list of clues.

What I usually do is create a table in Word (just like you see on the next page) in a document, and as I create a Concept Capsule, I type in the Capsule and then five clues for it just below.

I leave the extra black between the clues so that when I print and cut them out, I can make a good, even border.

You can also create these digitally (in Google Slides or similar). Do whatever works best for you! If you create them in Google Slides, I'd suggest changing the size of the slide to the same size as a piece of paper, in case you want to print them.

I print the clues on colored cardstock, cut the cards out, laminate them, and cut again.

Creating Taboo clues is an excellent opportunity for students who have mastered the vocabulary. It gives you a stronger ownership of the word when you have to consider what *not* to say. I often have students come up with better ideas than mine!

ELA:

ALLEGORY	ALLITERATION	ALLUSION	ANTAGONIST
HIDDEN MEANING	CONSONANT	REFER	OPPOSE
FABLE	FIRST	PERSON	PROTAGONIST
STORY	SOUND	PLACE	ENEMY
PERSON	LETTER	THING	AGAINST
ENTIRE	BEGIN	LITERATURE	ADVERSARY

IRONY	METAPHOR	ONOMATOPOEIA	PARADOX
DRAMATIC	COMPARE	SOUND	POSSIBLE
SITUATIONAL	TWO	POW	TRUE
VERBAL	LIKE	BAM	CONTRADICT
KNOW	SIMILAR	BOOM	CONTRARY
AUDIENCE	THINGS	COMIC	ABSURD

PERSONIFICATION	PROTAGONIST	SIMILE	THEME
HUMAN	MAIN	COMPARE	MAIN
THING	CHARACTER	TWO	IDEA
ANIMAL	MOVE	LIKE	ABOUT
IDEA	STORY	AS	STORY
FEELING	LEADING	THAN	MORAL

Math:

ACUTE ANGLE	ANGLE	COMPOSITE NUMBER	DIAMETER
LESS	TWO	FACTOR	ACROSS
MEASURES	RAYS	PRIME	CIRCLE
90	DEGREES	WHOLE	WIDEST
DEGREES	CORNER	TWO	SEGMENT
RANGE	COMMON	DIVISIBLE	DISTANCE

DIVIDEND	HISTOGRAM	IMPROPER FRACTION	ISOSCELES TRIANGLE
NUMBER	GRAPH	NUMERATOR	TWO
DIVIDED	RANGES	DENOMINATOR	CONGRUENT
INSIDE	BIN	GREATER	SIDES
DIVISOR	BAR	EQUAL	ANGLES
QUOTIENT	DATA	ONE	SAME

MEAN	MODE	OBTUSE ANGLE	PERIMETER
AVERAGE	MOST	MORE	AROUND
ADD	OFTEN	90	DISTANCE
DIVIDE	FREQUENT	DEGREES	SUM
CENTRAL	HIGHEST	LESS	CIRCUMFERENCE
X	ORDER	180	TWO

Science:

ABSORB	ADAPTATION	ANIMAL POPULATION	ARID
SOAK	MATCH	NUMBER	DRY
LIQUID	ENVIRONMENT	SPECIES	CLIMATE
PASS	BEHAVIOR	AREA	PRECIPITATION
ENERGY	BODY	LIMITING	XERIC
THROUGH	LONG	BREED	DESERT

BIOME	CARRYING CAPACITY	CHEMICAL CHANGE	CLOSED CIRCUIT
SPECIES	LIMIT	REACTION	COMPLETE
ANIMAL	ORGANISM	NEW	LOOP
PLANT	POPULATION	SUBSTANCE	ELECTRICITY
ADAPT	AVAILABILITY	PHYSICAL	CONDUCTOR
LIVING	ECOSYSTEM	HEAT	SOURCE

CONDENSATION	CONDUCTIVITY	CONSUMER	CORE
WATER	ELECTRIC	EAT	CENTER
VAPOR	CHARGE	ORGANISMS	EARTH
LIQUID	FLOW	PRIMARY	HOT
CYCLE	PHYSICAL	SECONDARY	LIQUID
EVAPORATION	SIEMENS	HETEROTROPH	SOLID

Social Studies:

ABSOLUTE LOCATION	COMPASS ROSE	CULTURE	DELTA
PLACE	CARDINAL	WAY	TRIANGLE
FIXED	DIRECTION	LANGUAGE	RIVER
LATITUDE	WIND	RELIGION	MOUTH
LONGITUDE	4	CUSTOMS	SILT
RELATIVE	MAP	DRESS	DEPOSIT

DEMOCRACY	GLACIER	LATITUDE	LONGITUDE
RIGHTS	DENSE	EAST	NORTH
ELECTED	ICE	WEST	SOUTH
FREE	FLOW	EQUATOR	PRIME MERIDIAN
ACCOUNTABLE	SNOW	DEGREES	DEGREES
LAW	LAND	LONGITUDE	LATITUDE

OASIS	PLACE	RELATIVE LOCATION	VOLCANO
FERTILE	PHYSICAL	PLACES	MOUNTAIN
DESERT	HUMAN	LANDMARKS	MAGMA
WATER	CHARACTERISTICS	POINTS	LAVA
AQUIFER	CHANGE	DIFFERENT	ERUPTIONS
TRADE	LIKE	ABSOLUTE	FLOW

ZAP! Board

ZAP! boards are a little bit labor intensive to make. They can be re-used again and again, so I don't mind. If you read through these directions and realize that you don't want to do all of this, simply print out the cards and use them in a deck, rather than on the board.

- To make a ZAP! board, first print the scoring cards on cardstock in color or black and white (https://www.giftedguru.com/zap-game-printable). Cut them out.

- Put the cards inside pockets glued or taped to a poster board.

- You can use the pockets that are designed for library cards. These are available at any craft store (and sometimes even the dollar store!).

If you want to make your own, simply search "printable library card holder template."

I find the pockets quite labor intensive to make, so I prefer to just buy them (they are only a few dollars). To make the board even more long-lasting, laminate the pockets and cut a slit in them at the pocket with an Exacto® knife. You know, this is the stuff they should teach you in college!

Label the board ZAP! using a marker (or simply cut out and glue on the label I've provided below).

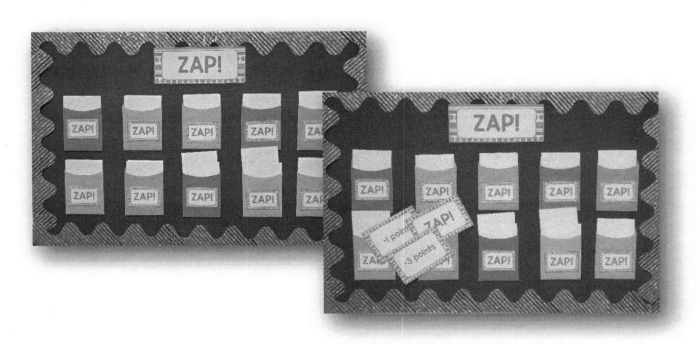

Acknowledgements

The only person besides the author who knows the blood, sweat, and tears that went into a book is the person's spouse. It may be an overused phrase, but it is still true that I could not have done it without the support of my husband, Steven. He has been there as I rummaged through my old teaching files, and he's expressed (feigned?) genuine interest as I found decades-old quizzes and samples, waving them in the air with glee. He's listened patiently as I've run ideas by him, and he never acts as though it gets old. He celebrates every book as if it's my first. Thank you.

This book would not have been written were it not for a conversation with my colleague Ian Byrd. At the time, we were just meeting to chat general business, but then he asked me if I realized how much interest there was in my vocabulary instruction ideas, and specifically the Concept Capsules. He said, "If you had a book, people would want it." I'm grateful for his belief in me that I could write another book so soon after the book he and I wrote together. He is also the source of frequent photos of his adorable son who brightens my day on many occasions. Sometimes he even sends them without my asking.

I have a group of colleagues in my field who are always there to listen and bounce ideas off of who deserve special thanks.

Brian Housand, my favorite cousin, not only gives great advice and insight, but he has got a wit to go with it that makes every conversation a pleasure. Brian's only fault is that he does not live closer because there is nothing that energizes me more than being with Brian and his wonderful wife Angela in person. Brian was one of the first people in the education community who made me feel like I had a place at the table. He was there for my very first conference keynote speech, and as I sat down, he whispered, "You hit it out of the park." I have never forgotten those words of encouragement.

Laurie Westphal's understanding of educational publishing has aided (and abetted!) me in innumerable ways. She is encouraging and practical – a rare and valuable combination.

Rebecca Archer and I met when we were teaching across the hall from each other, and she is a source of continuing inspiration to me. In addition to allowing me to reorganize her class bookcases and play with bulletin boards, she shares her pedagogical ideas with me, and keeps drawing me back to what's important: the students. Everyone wishes their child had a teacher like her.

Andrew McBurney is as close as I come to a teacher crush. He is a genius educator, the deepest thinker I know, and one of the few people who read me under the table. If life should ever decide to get fair, I'll teach down the hall from him someday.

Chris Hendricks is my teaching avatar. Every idea I have for classrooms, I run pass the Chris test, which is, "Would Chris think this were cool?" He is a daily reminder of how hard so many teachers are working to make life better, truly better, for kids. His enthusiasm and openness to new ideas are a constant inspiration.

Everything I do comes back in some way to my best friend of 35 years, Patricia Bear, to whom this book is dedicated. She manages to think the best of me at all times, and she believes in me even when I am full of doubt. There has never been a better friend.